THE
SECOND TRIVIA
QUIZBOOK

THE SECOND TRIVIA QUIZBOOK

GILBERT DAVIES

DRAKE PUBLISHERS INC.
NEW YORK · LONDON

Published in 1977 by
Drake Publishers, Inc.
801 Second Avenue
New York, N.Y. 10017

The Second Trivia Quizbook
LC: 76-55050

ISBN: 0-8473-1507-X

Printed in the United States of America

CONTENTS

THE
SECOND TRIVIA
QUIZBOOK

Questions

1. ADVERTISING SLOGANS

How many times have you dipped into a box of chocolate bonbons and wondered what flavor was hiding beneath the covering? Through trial and error most people have learned that a square means a caramel, an oblong a molasses chip, and, because of the shape, no one can mistake a chocolate cherry. But not every square turns out to be a caramel, and an oblong might be a nougat, but little raised ripples, lines, letters, dots, and other markings on the chocolate coverings have an advertised meaning all their own. Although no one seems to know exactly how or when this system of identifying chocolate-covered confections started, it probably dates back to the time when hand-dipped confections first appeared on the scene. Each chocolate maker seems to have developed his own marks as a practical way of making up the assortments that are then placed in fancifully decorated boxes. Throughout the years some of the same shapes and markings were adopted by a number of candy makers. Today, however, modern technology has stepped in, and the signs and symbols are disappearing along with the hand-dipped chocolates.

Many advertising slogans also come and go with time. In this chapter you are to match the slogan with that item it represented. Try for at least 99 44/100%!

Part I

1. A little dab'll do you
2. At the sign of the flying red horse
3. Better things for better living—through chemistry
4. Built like a skyscraper
5. Covers the earth
6. Eventually—why not now?
7. Hammer the Hammer
8. It's toasted
9. Often a bridesmaid, never a bride
10. The quality is remembered long after the price is forgotten
11. The racer's edge
12. So complete, all you add is love
13. They satisfy
14. Time to retire
15. When it rains, it pours

A. Lucky Strike cigarettes
B. Gold Medal flour
C. Morton's salt
D. Listerine
E. Chesterfield cigarettes
F. Shaw-Walker letter files
G. Brylcreem
H. Fisk tires
I. Simmons tools
J. Sherwin-Williams paints
K. Mobil gasoline
L. Iver Johnson revolvers
M. STP oil additive
N. Purina Dog Chow
O. DuPont

Part II

1. Ask the man who owns one
2. Avoid five o'clock shadow
3. Breakfast of Champions
4. Charcoal-mellowed, drop by drop
5. Does she—or doesn't she?
6. Fifty-seven varieties
7. It leaves you breathless
8. The light that never fails
9. Progress is our most important product
10. The quality goes in before the name goes on
11. Regular as clockwork
12. The tidy red tin
13. Think
14. The watch that made the dollar famous
15. You just know she wears them

A. Ingersoll
B. Heinz
C. General Electric
D. Wheaties
E. Packard automobile
F. Metropolitan Life Insurance
G. Nujol Oil laxative
H. McCallum hosiery
I. International Business Machines
J. Jack Daniel's whiskey
K. Clairol hair color
L. Gem razors
M. Zenith
N. Smirnoff vodka
O. Prince Albert smoking tobacco

2. ANIMAL CLASSIFICATION

Authorities differ on which snake possesses the most toxic venom. That of the 4'-to-5'-long tawny, dark-banded Australian tiger snake is perhaps matched by that of the blue drait of southeastern Asia and may be surpassed by the *Bothrops insularis*, found only on the island of Queimada Grande off southeastern Brazil. The tiger snake has a minimal lethal dose of 2 mg, or 1/14,000 ounce.

Cobras can use their deadly poison in two ways. They can bite with their poison fangs, which are in the front of the upper jaw, and some kinds can also squirt the poison directly at the eyes of the victim. In these kinds the fangs are shaped so that the poison is sent forward when the cobra tilts its head back. This is called spitting and is most highly developed in two African and one East Indian cobra. When the venom is spit out, it is not harmful to a man unless it gets in his eyes. It causes severe irritation and even blindness if it is not washed out immediately. The bite can cause death in a few hours.

Most of us know that rattlesnakes are also poisonous but are not aware that nature has equipped these snakes with organs called pits, which enable them to "see" in the dark. These organs on the sides of the head respond to heat rays. On the darkest of nights the snake can sense a mouse or squirrel because of the heat of its body.

In this chapter you don't have to worry about being poisoned, squirted, or seen in the dark. Match the orders with the animals. Remember that an order is a part of a class, which in turn is part of a phylum.

Order	Animal
Part I	
1. Insectivora	A. Dog
2. Ratita	B. Mole
3. Squamata	C. Snake
4. Carnivora	D. Ostrich
5. Cetacea	E. Whale
Part II	
1. Edentata	A. Grasshopper
2. Malacostraca	B. Trout
3. Primates	C. Monkey
4. Teleostoma	D. Anteater
5. Orthoptera	E. Shrimp
Part III	
1. Diptera	A. Kangaroo
2. Chelonia	B. Pig
3. Marsupialia	C. Elephant
4. Artiodactyla	D. Mosquito
5. Proboscidea	E. Turtle

3. ANIMAL COLLECTIVES OR GROUPS

How much honey does a bee collect, and how do bees keep warm in the winter? Do all lobsters have their heavy claws on the same side? Are blindworms actually blind? First things first.

A bee does not actually collect honey but nectar, which it converts into honey. An average hive containing 2,000 bees produces about 20 pounds of honey a year, thus in a year a single bee would produce about 1/100 pound of honey. Bees keep warm inside the hive by clustering together. The queen is near the center. The bees on the inside of the cluster make heat by moving rapidly about, and from time to time they change places with those on the inside. In this way all the bees can rest and warm themselves. On a very cold day the center of the bee cluster may be 75 degrees warmer than the outer air.

All lobsters do not have the heavy claw on the same side. Some are "right-handed," and others "left-handed." The heavy claw has blunt teeth to crush its prey, and the smaller claw has sharp teeth to tear the prey to pieces.

The blindworm is a common name for two different groups of animals, which have small eyes and no legs. They are not blind, however, nor are they worms. One group is amphibians, related to frogs, toads, and salamanders; the other group is lizards and belongs to the class of reptiles.

In this chapter you are to match the name of the animal with the name of its collective or group — such as a school of fish.

Name of Animal	Name of Group
	Part I
1. Apes	A. Band
2. Badgers	B. Cete
3. Elephants	C. Crash
4. Foxes	D. Dray (or drey)
5. Gorillas	E. Flock
6. Kangaroos	F. Herd
7. Lions	G. Pod
8. Rhinoceros	H. Pride
9. Seals	I. Shrewdness
10. Sheep	J. Skulk
11. Squirrels	K. Sounder
12. Swine	L. Troop
	Part II
1. Coots	A. Bevy
2. Crows	B. Covert
3. Geese	C. Gaggle
4. Herons	D. Murder
5. Nightingales	E. Nye (or nide)

6. Pheasants		F.	Muster
7. Quails		G.	Rafter
8. Peacocks		H.	Sedge (or siege)
9. Ravens		I.	Unkindness
10. Turkeys		J.	Watch
11. Larks		K.	Sord
12. Mallards		L.	Exaltation

4. ANIMAL YOUNG

Although man ranks first among the mammals in length of life, the turtle lives longer than any animal. It has been proven to live more than 150 years. After man among the mammals, comes the elephant, which can live from 45 to 70 years, followed by the rhinoceros, which lives from 36 to 50 years. Gorillas sometimes live 35 years, whales more than 30, horses 20 to 35, lions 20 to 30, cats 7 to 15, and dogs 5 to 15. The most durable fish is the carp, one of which is known to have reached the age of 75. An occasional parrot lives to be 60. Many adult insects live only an hour or two, but queen ants may reign as long as 16 years. The turtle, however, has no real competition among the reptiles: the alligator record is 43; the oldest known snake died at 21.

This quiz is about the young of animals. Match the animal with the common name for the young of the species.

Animal	**Young of Animal**
1. Cow	A. Cheeper
2. Deer	B. Cockerel
3. Eel	C. Colt
4. Goat	D. Cygnet
5. Goose	E. Elver
6. Hare	F. Fawn
7. Hen	G. Filly
8. Female horse	H. Gosling
9. Male horse	I. Heifer
10. Kangaroo	J. Joey
11. Partridge	K. Kid
12. Pigeon	L. Lamb
13. Rooster	M. Leveret
14. Salmon	N. Parr
15. Seal	O. Poult
16. Sheep	P. Pullet
17. Swan	Q. Pup
18. Turkey	R. Squab (or squeaker)

5. ANTHROPOLOGY LANGUAGE

Very few new vegetables have been introduced in historic times, and in many cases little improvement has been made on the products of the ancients. Lettuce never has been found wild. It is believed to have first been cultivated in India or Central Asia. Herodotus, Hippocrates, and Aristotle mention it in references to Greek gardens. Celery is a biennial plant native to the marshlands of southern Europe, North Africa, and southwestern Asia. It was long considered poisonous and was not eaten until modern times. Pumpkins and squashes were grown in America long before Europeans came on the scene. Peas are the oldest known vegetables. They are believed to have originated in Ethiopia and spread over Europe and Asia. They were eaten and possibly cultivated in Europe during the Stone Age. Columbus planted them in the West Indies in 1493, and they spread rapidly among the Indians and became one of the chief crops of the Iroquois. The species from which cabbage is derived grows wild in North Africa and along the European shore of the Mediterranean. It has been cultivated for 4,000 years. The turnip is a native of western and central China. The radish is a native of China and India. It was cultivated by both the Greeks and the Egyptians. The parsnip, another Asiatic root crop, was first planted in Virginia in 1690. Popcorn, of course, is peculiarly American. In early Spanish writings reference is made to an Aztec ritual in which "one hour before dawn there sallied forth all these maidens crowned with garlands of maize, toasted and popped, the grains of which were like orange blossoms — and on their necks thick festoons of the same which passed under the left arm."

This chapter can be tried before or after meals. Match the definitions to the correct words in both parts.

Part I

1. The scientific description and formulation of sounds employed in language
2. Highly conventionalized written characters that are a later development of picture writing
3. A custom found in many areas in which the husband observes special taboos, restrictions, or other confining behavior for a number of days after his wife gives birth
4. A type of consonant sound exemplified by ts or dz
5. A term used for peoples who change their area of residence seasonally within a larger domain that is their home country
6. A written character or symbol for a word
7. The belief in individual spiritual beings, found among all primitive economies
8. The social relationship in which there are especially close ties between a nephew and his uncle
9. The reckoning of group membership or descent through the father rather than the mother

10. Belief in plural deities
11. Living together in more or less intimate association
12. An economic system in which production of or with domesticated animals constitutes a major economic resource
13. Cannibalism
14. A clan society in which each half of the community may include one or more interconnected clans
15. The hereditary protrusion of the upper jaw

WORD LIST

A. Affricative	F. Hieroglyph	K. Patrilineal
B. Animism	G. Ideograph	L. Phonetics
C. Anthropophagy	H. Moiety	M. Polytheism
D. Avunculate	I. Nomad	N. Prognathism
E. Couvade	J. Pastoralism	O. Symbiotic

Part II

1. The primate suborder that evolved in the Tertiary period and that includes monkeys, apes, and humans
2. An object to which supernatural potency is ascribed
3. A member of any Pleistocene species on the human line of ascent
4. A term used for any society in which the female sex has lower status
5. Polynesian people who reside in New Zealand
6. A giving-away feast characteristic of the Pacific Northwest Coast
7. The Polynesian name for a type of cloth made of beaten bark
8. A figure, design, or symbol cut into rock
9. The independent development of similar features of culture — for example, similar geometric basketry designs that are historically unconnected
10. The social relationship in which there are especially close ties between a niece and her aunt
11. Anything such as a tool, container, weapon, garment, or ornament that is made by human hands
12. An especially pronounced deposition of fat on the buttocks
13. The last 500,000 to 1,000,000 or more years of geological history until the end of the last glacial period
14. The first Tertiary geological epoch, during which lemurs and tarsiers appeared
15. A minimal unit composed of one or several sounds of distinguishable meaning and function

WORD LIST

A. Amitate	F. Homonid	K. Petroglyph
B. Anthropoid	G. Maori	L. Pleistocene
C. Artifact	H. Morpheme	M. Potlatch
D. Convergence	I. Paleocene	N. Steatopygy
E. Fetish	J. Patriarchate	O. Tapa

6. ASTRONOMY LANGUAGE

One October morning in 1937 a German astronomer at Konigstuhl Observatory found a faint white line on one of the photographic plates exposed to the heavens the previous night. Obviously some unexpected object was hurtling through the sky much closer to the earth than the slow-moving stars. The length and curvature of the streak suggested to Dr. Karl Reinmuth that the object was an asteroid or planetoid — one of the baby planets that circle the sun along with their giant brothers. The evidence also indicated that the object was passing rather close to the earth. Additional observations found on plates at Johannesburg and Harvard told astronomers some interesting facts about this asteroid, which was named Hermes. They learned that it was about one mile in diameter and that it circled the sun approximately once every two years. But the remarkable thing about Hermes was that it had passed within 500,000 miles of the earth. This put Hermes in the category of an astronomical near-miss and made it the closest of all the asteroids. One British astronomer estimated that in its future travels Hermes might even come within 220,000 miles of the earth, a bit closer than the moon. Unfortunately, it has never been possible to check the accuracy of such computations by further observations of the asteroid. Traveling at its phenomenal speed, it was quickly lost in the far reaches of the solar system and has never been found again.

Hermes is by no means unique. The great majority of the little planets picked up at one time or another on photographic plates have also slipped from further view. This is true, for example, of both Adonis and Apollo, the second and third closest asteroids. Adonis was estimated to have approached within 1,376,000 miles of the earth in 1936, and Apollo came within 3,000,000 miles in 1932.

Whether you are slow or fast, large or small, try your hand at matching the definitions to the words in both parts of this chapter.

Part I

1. The outermost portion of the sun's atmosphere
2. The name of one of the satellites of Uranus
3. A meteor bright enough to cast a shadow
4. A meteoroid that explodes in the air
5. Points at which the planes of the orbits of two celestial bodies intersect
6. The interval of time that passes between the occurrence of eclipses at or near the same place upon the surface of the earth
7. The passage of an apparently small body across the face of an apparently large body
8. Approximately 3.26 light years
9. A star in what is believed to be the last stages of stellar evolution

10. A cloudlike, luminous mass composed of gaseous matter or of stars far beyond the solar system
11. The name given to a region of the southern sky adjacent to the Southern Cross in which a cloud of cosmic dust hides the light of many stars
12. The name for the group of seven bright stars in the constellation of Ursa Major, or the Big Dipper

WORD LIST

A. Bolide	E. Fireball	I. Parsec
B. Charles's Wain	F. Miranda	J. Saros
C. Coalsack	G. Nebula	K. Transit
D. Corona	H. Nodes	L. White dwarf

Part II

1. Bright clouds, usually made of calcium, which are found on the sun near sunspots and which are sometimes called plages
2. A fragment of stony or metallic material in space
3. Meteors associated with a meteor shower that has not been observed for a number of years
4. The measure of the ability of a body to reflect light from its surface
5. A number of bright points of light that can be seen for a few seconds at the instant of a total eclipse of the sun
6. The occurrence in which one body, because of size or position, hides from the earth's view another body that is or appears to be smaller than the concealing body
7. The partial or imperfect shadow outside the complete shadow of an opaque body in which the light from the source of illumination is only partly cut off
8. The measure of the brightness of a star or of any luminous body in the heavens
9. A seemingly though not actually new star that flares up and gradually grows fainter
10. A star whose brightness varies in a regular period of time because of some intrinsic quality in its physical makeup
11. A group of stars within a specific region
12. Two small, irregular galaxies that are the nearest of the outer galaxies to our own Milky Way

WORD LIST

A. Albedo	E. Constellation	I. Meteroid
B. Baily's Beads	F. Flocculi	J. Nova
C. Bielids	G. Magellanic clouds	K. Occultation
D. Cepheid	H. Magnitude	L. Penumbra

7. ASTRONOMY - TRUE/FALSE

To the unaided eye the bright surface of the moon is marred by vague dark areas. Through a low-powered telescope these dark areas appear as smooth plains, so uniform that early astronomers thought that they might be seas. With more powerful telescopes the smoothness of the "seas" is found to be only relative. Other parts of the lunar landscape appear to be very rugged, with numerous mountains and other formations. The so-called seas, mountains, craters, rills, and rays make up the principal features of the lunar landscape. Riccioli, an Italian astronomer who mapped the moon in the 17th century, named the craters for men of science. He also gve the seas such fanciful names as Mare Tranquillitatis (Sea of Tranquility) and Mare Serenitatis (Sea of Serenity). Similarly, many lunar mountain ranges are named after ranges on the earth, such as the Apennines, Caucasus, and Alps. The mountains are seen mostly in chains or groups, with single peaks as high as 29,000'. The Apennine range consists of some 3,000 peaks extending about 400 miles and rising some 18,000' above the Sea of Showers. A particular feature of the Alps is a great gorge, some 80 miles long and 4 to 6 miles wide. The rills are narrow crevices from as little as 10 to over 300 miles long, less than a few miles wide, and of unknown depth. Although inconspicuous because of their width, over a thousand rills have been located. In contrast, the rays are narrow streaks that are lighter in color than their surroundings and that radiate from several prominent craters, notably Tycho, Copernicus, and Kepler. Since they cast no shadows, they can be neither ridges or crevices. The rays that center on Copernicus extend hundreds of miles across the landscape. The most numerous of the lunar-landscape features are the craters. As far back as 1878 around 32,000 craters were mapped. The craters are roughly circular in shape, with the floor generally lower than the surrounding plain. Many contain mountains rising from their floors; in others numerous smaller craters are found.

You have a 50% chance in this chapter even if you guess. Decide if the statements are true or false.

1. The sun is a star
2. The sun is more than 100 times the diameter of the earth
3. Less than half of the known elements are found in the sun
4. Sunspots are hotter than the rest of the sun
5. The earth's average speed around the sun is less than 20 miles per second
6. The moon has no effect on weather
7. All known satellites revolve around their planets in the same direction
8. The planet Mercury is smaller than the planet Venus
9. The planet Venus has an atmosphere
10. A day on Mars is shorter than a day on earth
11. The mass of Jupiter is larger than the masses of all the other planets put together
12. It takes more than 10 of our years for Jupiter to travel around the sun
13. Two of Jupiter's satellites are larger than Mercury
14. Although Saturn's diameter is 9 times the diameter of the earth, its mass is only 95.3 times the mass of the earth
15. All asteroids revolve about the sun in a belt that lies between the orbits of Mars and Jupiter
16. The word "comet" is from the Latin word *coma,* which means "hair"
17. The tail of a comet usually points toward the sun
18. Meteorites are meteoroids that have landed upon the earth
19. When a planet or the moon is on the same side of the earth as the sun, it is said to be in conjunction
20. It is possible to have two lunar eclipses and five solar eclipses in a single year
21. Proxima Centauri is the star nearest the earth
22. All the stars in space combine to send to the earth an amount of light greater than the light of the full moon
23. When viewed by the naked eye and telescopes, stars have colors such as red, orange, yellow, white, blue, violet, and green
24. The shape of the orbit of any celestial body is an ellipse
25. The solar system is closer to the center of our galaxy than to the edge

8. BIOLOGY LANGUAGE

Hypertension, which is the medical name for high blood pressure and its complicated relative, atherosclerosis, is often the real villain behind strokes, apoplexy, heart failure, uremia, and coronary heart disease. Anyone who has had a medical examination knows how blood pressure is determined, but not everyone knows the name of the apparatus that the doctor uses — the sphygmomanometer.

Around the patient's arm the physician slips a fabric cuff containing a rubber bag connected to a hand bulb and a pressure gauge. He inflates the cuff until the arm's main artery is squeezed tightly enough to shut off the flow of blood. By placing his fingers on the pulse at the wrist or by listening with his stethoscope placed over the artery the doctor can tell when the flow ceases, for the pulse disappears. He then slowly deflates the cuff. As the pressure of the cuff against the artery is released, he takes a reading at the point when the pulse can first be heard or felt. This is the systolic pressure — the maximum pressure in the arteries when the heart is contracting. This pressure, measured in terms of the height of the column of mercury that it will support, may read 120mm, 130, 140, or more.

The physician continues to deflate the cuff and takes a reading at the moment when the sound disappears as the heart begins its fractional second of rest before its next contraction. This is the diastolic pressure — the minimum pressure maintained in the arteries between heartbeats. This reading is smaller, usually enough to sustain 80 to 90mm of mercury. The two readings are expressed as a fraction, with systolic pressure over diastolic — 130/90, for example.

Don't get your blood pressure up if you can't match the definitions with the words in both parts of this chapter.

Part I

1. The red coloring matter of blood that carries oxygen
2. A young, partly developed animal in its earliest stage of growth inside the mother
3. A changed heredity characteristic caused by changes in the genes
4. The process of producing protoplasm from digested foods
5. An animal possessing a backbone
6. An arthropod with eight legs and two body divisions
7. The early wormlike stage of an insect, which undergoes metamorphosis
8. The living, active part of every cell
9. An organism differing from its species because of a lack of color
10. The outer layer of cells in a living organism
11. A tiny vessel that connects an artery with a vein
12. An organism that lives upon dead organic matter

13. A small particle found in chromosomes that transmits heredity traits
14. Green-colored material in plants
15. Egg and sperm cells
16. The process by which green plants manufacture carbohydrates

WORD LIST

A.	Albino	I.	Gene
B.	Arachnid	J.	Hemoglobin
C.	Assimilation	K.	Larva
D.	Capillary	L.	Mutation
E.	Chlorophyll	M.	Photosynthesis
F.	Embryo	N.	Protoplasm
G.	Epidermis	O.	Saprophyte
H.	Gametes	P.	Vertebrate

Part II

1. A group containing such plants as mosses and liverworts
2. A mass of nerve-cell bodies
3. A small, definite-shaped bit of protoplasm in the nucleus of a cell, which transmits hereditary characteristics
4. A fertilized egg
5. Having parents of unlike groups
6. An invertebrate animal with jointed legs
7. The part of the flower in which the ovary is located
8. The tip of a stamen in a flower
9. Algae and fungus growing together and dependent upon each other
10. An animal or plant that lives in or on another living thing from which it obtains its food
11. A material that causes a chemical change in an organism
12. A pollen-producing organ of a flower
13. Flesh-eating mammals
14. A subdivision of a family — part of a classification
15. A simple plant containing no chlorophyll
16. Tiny, one-celled animals

WORD LIST

A.	Anther	I.	Genus
B.	Arthropod	J.	Hybrid
C.	Bryophyta	K.	Lichen
D.	Carnivora	L.	Parasite
E.	Chromosome	M.	Pistil
F.	Enzymes	N.	Protozoan
G.	Fungus	O.	Stamen
H.	Ganglion	P.	Zygote

9. BIRDS

There are several theories as to why birds migrate. One is that in earlier ages nonmigratory birds swarmed over the entire Northern Hemisphere, which at that time afforded a plentiful year-long food supply, such as now exists only in the tropics. Gradually, however, the glacial ice fields pushed southward, forcing the birds before them until finally all bird life was concentrated in the southern latitudes. As ages passed, the ice cap gradually retreated, and each spring the birds whose ancentral home had formerly been in the North tried to return there, only to be driven south again at the approach of winter. As the size of the ice-covered area decreased, the journeys northward became longer. Eventually the climatic conditions of our present age were establish-ed, and the birds continue the habit of migration, flying north in the summer to raise their young and returning to the southland when winter has cut off their food supply.

An opposing theory proposes that the ancestral home of all birds was in the tropics and that as this area became overpopulated, many species were gradually forced northward to find food and breeding grounds, only to be forced southward again by the annual recurrence of winter. Gradually, as the glacial ice retreated, vast areas of virgin country became suitable for summer occupancy, but the winter habitat in the South remained the home to which the birds returned after the nesting season.

Both of these theories assume that migration is an ingrained habit, but both have been criticized on biological and geological grounds, so neither should be accepted without qualification.

You don't have to move to try the three parts of this chapter: match old-time names with modern names; person's names with bird names; and mean-ing with ornithological term.

Part I

Old-Time	Modern
1. Bartram's sandpiper	A. Black vulture
2. Butcher-bird	B. Bobolink
3. Carolina pigeon	C. Mourning dove
4. Carrion crow	D. Painted bunting
5. Cock-of-the-plains	E. Peregrine falcon
6. Golden-winged woodpecker	F. Rufous-sided towhee
7. Great-footed hawk	G. Sage grouse
8. Ground robin	H. Shrike
9. Nonpareil	I. Upland plover
10. Rice bunting	J. Yellow-shafter flicker

Part II

Person	Bird
1. Audubon's	A. Blackbrid
2. Baird's	B. Gull
3. Bonaparte's	C. Hawk
4. Brewer's	D. Jay
5. Clark's	E. Nutcracker
6. Cooper's	F. Phoebe
7. Forster's	G. Quail
8. Gambel's	H. Sparrow
9. Say's	I. Tern
10. Steller's	J. Warbler

Part III

1. Abnormal absence of color	A. Albinism
2. Back of the neck	B. Auriculars
3. Feathers around the ear	C. Axillars
4. Flight feathers	D. Erythrism
5. Spaces between eyes and bill	E. Lores
6. Tail feathers	F. Melanism
7. Two toes forward, two toes back	G. Nape
8. Wing-pit feathers	H. Rectrices
9. With an excess of black coloration	I. Primaries
10. With an excess of red coloration	J. Zygodactyl

10. CHEMISTRY LANGUAGE

In 1635 John Winthrop the Younger, governor of Connecticut and an amateur mineralogist, came across a fragment of strange rock. It was sent by his grandson to London, and in 1801 the English chemist Charles Hatchett detected in the rock element number 41, which he named columbium in honor of the country in whose territory the mineral was first discovered. In 1802 the Swedish chemist Ekeberg discovered the element tantalum. Because columbium and tantalum were chemically very similar, the English chemist William Hyde Wollaston decided in 1809 that the two were identical. If they were identical, then Hatchett's name columbium should have prevailed, since he was first. But Berzelius, Europe's leading chemist, thought Ekeberg's work more thorough and convincing and in 1814 voted against columbium and for tantalum.

In 1846 the German chemist Heinrich Rose showed that columbium and tantalum were two different elements. Because of their similarity Rose called columbium niobium after Niobe, the daughter of Tantalus. The element kept its two names for many years — columbium in the United States and niobium in Europe. In recent times, however, an international conference of chemists decided to make niobium the official name of the element.

It is hoped that you won't have the same problem in matching the elements and their symbols and the definitions and their meanings.

Part I

1. Antimony	A. Ag
2. Gold	B. Au
3. Iron	C. Fe
4. Lead	D. Hg
5. Mercury	E. K
6. Potassium	F. Na
7. Silver	G. Pb
8. Sodium	H. Sb
9. Tin	I. Sn
10. Tungsten	J. W

Part II

1. An insoluble solid that separates from a solution
2. A substance consisting entirely of atoms of the same atomic number

3. A homogeneous substance composed of two or more chemical elements, the proportions of which are fixed and invariable by weight
4. A solution of two or more metals
5. The formation of a compound from its elements or from simpler compounds
6. The smallest unit of an element or compound that can exist by itself in a free state
7. A solid in which the component molecules, atoms, or ions are oriented in a definite and repeated geometric pattern
8. An atom or group of atoms possessing an electrical charge
9. A group of atoms that functions as a unit in chemical change
10. A substance that alters the rate at which a chemical reaction takes place but itself remains unchanged
11. Vaporization and subsequent condensation of a liquid
12. Diffusion of a solvent through a semipermeable membrane into a more concentrated solution
13. A number that represents the combining power of an atom or radical in terms of hydrogen as a standard
14. Molecules that have the same number and kinds of atoms but different molecular configurations
15. Chemical decomposition of a substance by water in which the water itself is also decomposed
16. Dispersion of minute droplets of one liquid, which does not dissolve, in another
17. Dispersion in a medium of particles that are aggregates of molecules
18. Organic compounds that correspond to inorganic salts and are derived by replacing the hydrogen in an acid by an organic radical or group

WORD LIST

A. Alloy
B. Catalyst
C. Colloid
D. Compound
E. Crystal
F. Distillation
G. Element
H. Emulsion
I. Ester
J. Hydrolysis
K. Ion
L. Isomers
M. Molecule
N. Osmosis
O. Precipitate
P. Radical
Q. Synthesis
R. Valence

11. CHEMISTRY MULTIPLE-CHOICE

Insects are curious little beasts, the oldest on earth. They have skittered and buzzed around for some 300 million years, and today, despite poisons and flyswatters, they still number nine out of every ten of the earth's creatures. Given its way, the insect would steal man's food and fiber and endanger his health. But man has attempted to control the insect, largely with the use of poisons.

Now man has chosen to set aside his strongest weapons — the persistent pesticides such as DDT, so once again he is faced with wormy apples and crop diseases. Man has employed every possible means of overkill from the heel of his boot to the flat of his hand, from aircraft to sound effects. But the odds, as always, are with the bugs. Take two houseflies, for instance. If they and their progeny bred successfully, they would produce 190 quintillion flies in just four months. Of course, birds, disease, and other natural enemies keep this from happening. Or take a flight of locusts attacking a wheat field. They might weigh as much as 50,000 tons, the combined weight of 250 B-52 jet bombers loaded for war, and in a single day they would eat their own weight in wheat — enough to feed 5 million human beings. How to stop these insects and others like them? With more chemicals or with biological controls? That is a big question that is still unanswered.

This chapter offers another type of chemistry choice. There are 20 questions with multiple-choice answers: pick the right one.

1. The elements Li, Na, K, Rb, and Cs are known as the
   a. Transition metals
   b. Alkali metals
   c. Alkaline earths
   d. Heavy metals
   e. Noble metals
2. Who discovered oxygen?
   a. Avogadro
   b. Boyle
   c. Cavendish
   d. Lavoisier
   e. Priestley
3. Which of the following is not an amino acid?
   a. Leucine
   b. Valine
   c. Choline
   d. Lysine
   e. Alanine

4. Check the incorrect statement
   a. Ozone is more active than oxygen
   b. Ozone is produced by the electrolysis of water
   c. Ozone has a pungent odor
   d. Ozone is used for deodorizing, disinfecting, and bleaching purposes
   e. Ozone is an allotropic form of oxygen
5. Check the incorrect statement: the valence of an element is equal to
   a. the number of electrons gained or lost by the element in forming a compound
   b. the number of electrons shared by the reacting elements
   c. the charge of the ion formed by the element
   d. the difference between the number of protons and the number of neutrons in the nucleus
   e. the difference between the number of protons in the nucleus and the number of electrons outside the nucleus
6. Check the correct statement
   a. Electrons are present in the nucleus
   b. The atomic number of an element is equal to the number of neutrons in the nucleus
   c. The atomic number of an element is equal to the number of valence electrons
   d. Neutrons have practically the same weight as protons
   e. The mass of an element is principally composed of electrons
7. Which of the following scientists had the most to do with the periodic table?
   a. Cavendish
   b. Madame Curie
   c. Lavoisier
   d. Mendeleev
   e. Priestley
8. Check the incorrect statement
   a. Water reacts with soluble metallic oxides to form bases
   b. Water reacts with nonmetallic oxides to form acids
   c. Water decomposes when heated to a high temperature
   d. Water forms hydrates with certain anhydrous salts
   e. Water reacts with active metals, liberating hydrogen
9. Ammonium hydroxide is a weak base because
   a. It does not ionize
   b. It has a small percentage of ionization
   c. It will not react with an acid
   d. It forms hydrogen ions in solution
   e. One mole of ammonium hydroxide will not neutralize one mole of acid

10. Which is not a factor in the solubility of a solid in water?
    a. Nature of the solute
    b. Temperature
    c. Pressure
    d. Surface of the solid
    e. Stirring (or agitation)
11. The one element that is present in all organic compounds is
    a. oxygen
    b. hydrogen
    c. carbon
    d. nitrogen
    e. sulfur
12. Which compound is an alkaloid?
    a. Niacin
    b. Quinine
    c. Adrenalin
    d. Aspirin
    e. Choline
13. Check the incorrect statement: a nonvolatile solute dissolved in water affects water in the following ways
    a. Lowers its vapor pressure
    b. Raises its boiling point
    c. Lowers its freezing point
    d. Lowers its osmotic pressure
    e. Raises its density
14. Which of the following accumulates in the muscle as a result of vigorous exercise?
    a. Muscle glycogen
    b. Lactic acid
    c. Glucose
    d. Carbon dioxide
    e. Amino acids
15. Oxygen is prepared in the laboratory by
    a. Decomposing water by heat
    b. Heating sand
    c. Heating potassium chlorate
    d. Heating nonmetallic oxides
    e. Reacting an acid with a base

16. What percentage of dry air is oxygen?
    a. 1%
    b. 21%
    c. 50%
    d. 75%
    e. 85%
17. A chemical bond formed by the sharing of electrons between the reacting atoms is known as
    a. an ionic bond
    b. a covalent bond
    c. a polar bond
    d. a dative bond
    e. an electrovalent bond
18. Which of the following will react with water to create an acidic solution?
    a. H^2
    b. SO^3
    c. CaO
    d. NH^3
    e. Na^2CO^3
19. A normal solution is one that contains
    a. One grammolecular weight of solute per liter of solution
    b. One grammolecular weight of solute per liter of solvent
    c. One gramequivalent weight per liter of solution
    d. One gramequivalent weight per liter of solvent
    e. One gramequivalent weight per 1,000 grams of solution
20. Which element is not present in all proteins?
    a. C
    b. H
    c. O
    d. N
    E. P

12. COLORS

The lightning bugs, or fireflies, that are seen so often on summer evenings are similar to a species of beetle called the flowworm in Great Britain. Only the female is the lightning bug, for the male is not equipped with any lighting power. He has the bad habit of going out at night, so the female has to make part of her body shine with a sort of phosphorus-green light in order to show him the way home, much as a dweller in a poorly lighted street keeps a light in the window or on the porch to guide visitors or the late homecomer to the proper house.

The most brilliant fireflies are found only in the warmer regions of the world. Fine print may be read by the light of one found in the West Indies. In Cuba ladies once had a fashion of imprisoning them in bits of netting or fine-textured lace and wearing them as dress ornaments, and in Haiti they are confined in a vial that emits sufficient light to enable a person to write or perform other domestic chores.

You should use a light bulb of some type in order to match the name of the color with its proper hue.

Part I

1. Mimosa
2. Terre-verte
3. Taupe
4. Algerian
5. Citrine
6. Heliotrope
7. Hyacinth
8. Russet

A. Reddish blue-red
B. Brownish gray
C. Light yellow
D. Reddish brown
E. Bluish blue-red
F. Tan bark
G. Bluish green
H. Reddish yellow

Part II

1. Jasmine
2. Email
3. Terracotta
4. Cerise
5. Tawny
6. Mauvette
7. Goya
8. Magenta

A. Green-blue
B. English vermilion
C. Deep purplish red
D. Cherry red
E. Light yellow
F. Reddish red-yellow
G. Blue-red
H. Brownish orange

13. COOKS IN THE KITCHEN

Long before the discovery of America cacao was cultivated as a food by the Aztecs. When Christopher Columbus reached the New World, he learned of cacao and took a few beans back to Spain as curios, though he knew nothing of their food value. A few years later in 1528 when Cortez of Spain invaded Mexico, the real value of cacao was discovered. The importance of cacao beans to the Aztecs may be judged by the fact that they were used as a means of exchange or currency. When Cortez returned to Spain, he brought back news of a drink that was entirely unknown in Europe. The drink was called *chocolatl* and was in common use among the Aztecs. The term "cocoa" is derived from cacao and is universally used in English-speaking countries to designate the seed of the cacao tree.

When Cortez first entered Mexico, the emperor Montezuma entertained him and his followers at a banquet at which the only beverage was chocolate flavored with vanilla and other spices, whipped to a froth, and served cold. Montezuma drank no other beverage: it was served to him in golden goblets and after each one was drained, it was thrown into the lake that surrounded the palace. At one feast he emptied 50 goblets, while his guards and attendants consumed 2,000 jarfuls.

After Cortez introduced cocoa into Spain, it soon became very popular, although the Spaniards endeavored to keep its preparation a secret. In 1606 it became known in Italy, from whence it spread to Austria and was introduced in France by Anne upon her marriage to Louis XIII.

Chocolate houses became popular in both England and Germany in the middle of the 17th century. Spain controlled the world source of cacao and gained great wealth from its sale. So high a price was maintained that the beverage was beyond the reach of any but the most wealthy.

Neither wealth nor a thirst is needed to answer the following questions about food, so try your gourmet knowhow.

1. What is meant by the cooking term "marinate"?
2. Name the condiment, made only in Louisiana, that has the name of a small river and state in southeast Mexico situated at the head of the Gulf of Campeche.
3. True or false: eggs separate more easily when they are very cold.
4. Robert Arthur Talbot Gascoyne-Cecil was the name of an English prime minister in the late 19th century. His title is used to describe which chopped-meat dish?
5. Bread is at its best for sandwiches when it is how old?
6. What is the fish appetizer named for the Iron Chancellor who helped found the German Republic?
7. How quickly after preparation should a souffle be served?
8. What food and drink does Robin Redbreast offer Jenny Wren in the rhyme?
9. Evaporated and condensed milk are both used in recipes. Which of the two products is already sweetened?
10. In *The Vicar of Wakefield,* a novel by Oliver Goldsmith, Mrs. Primrose, the vicar's wife, was famous for a beverage made from a berry. Name it.
11. Fish is enjoyed in every part of the world. In the United States which fish is usually referred to as "sole"?
12. Why did King Arthur steal three sacks of barley meal in the nursery rhyme?
13. A batter pudding baked under meat has the same name as the largest county in England. What is it?
14. What condiment is named for the English city in which Cromwell routed Charles II and the Scots in 1651 and achieved his final victory?
15. Name the country or region identified with the following native dishes:
    a. Goulash, a beef stew
    b. Bouillabaisse, a fish chowder
    c. Borscht, a beef soup
    d. Knockwurst, a sausage
    e. Minestrone, a vegetable soup
    f. Matjes herring, an immature female herring

14. COOK'S TOUR

The story of tea goes back so far that its true beginning is lost in time. Life was very simple and man had only a glimmering of his present-day knowledge when the Chinese Emperor Shen Nung knelt before a fire to boil water. Called the Divine Healer, the wise emperor always boiled water before drinking it. Nobody knew the causes of illnesses, but Shen Nung had observed that people who boiled their drinking water had better health. Shen Nung's servants made the fire from the branches of a nearby tree. As the water began to boil merrily, some of the topmost leaves of the branches fell into the boiling pot. "What a delightful aroma! exclaimed the emperor as the fragrance of tea floated on the air for the first time. He sipped the steaming liquid. "Ah! And what a flavor!" That, the Chinese will tell you, is how tea was discovered around 2737 B.C.

The people of India have another story about the origin of tea as a drink. Some 1,000 years ago a saintly Buddhist priest named Darma wanted to prove his faith. He decided to do so by spending seven years without sleep, thinking only of Buddha. For five years Darma thought of Buddha day and night. Then, to his dismay, he found himself falling asleep. Darma fought to keep his eyes open. In desperation he snatched a handful of leaves from a nearby bush and chewed them, hoping that they would keep him awake. The leaves, of course, were the leaves of the tea bush. Darma felt refreshed and awake after chewing them. With their help he was able to complete his seven years of meditation without once falling asleep.

It is hoped that you won't go to sleep when you attempt to choose the correct spelling of the cosmopolitan specialties below.

1.	a. Veal scalopine	b. Veal scalopini	c. Veal scaloppine
2.	a. Soufle	b. Souffle	c. Souflle
3.	a. Shallotts	b. Shallotts	c. Shalots
4.	a. Chutney	b. Chutny	c. Chutnay
5.	a. Minestrone	b. Ministrone	c. Menistrone
6.	a. Charlotte ruse	b. Charllote russ	c. Charlotte russe
7.	a. Beef strogonov	b. Beef stroganof	c. Beef Stroganoff
8.	a. Parfait	b. Parffait	c. Parfete
9.	a. Veal alla parmigiana	b. Veal ala parmegian	c. Veal alla parmigian
10.	a. Goulash	b. Goulash	c. Goulach
11.	a. Chili con carne	b. Chille con carne	c. Chili con carne
12.	a. Weiner shnitzel	b. Wiener shnitzel	c. Wiener schnitzel
13.	a. Enchilladas	b. Enchelladas	c. Enchiladas
14.	a. Sukyaka	b. Soukiyaki	c. Sukiyaki
15.	a. Chow mein	b. Chow mein	c. Chow meine
16.	a. Vichysoisse	b. Vichysoise	c. Vichyssoise
17.	a. Crepe susettes	b. Crepes suzette	c. Crepes susette
18.	a. Hors d'oeuvres	b. Hor d'euvres	c. Hors d'oeuvres

15. DRUG SLANG

Although the question has often been asked whether psychedelic drugs prod the brain into initiating new ideas that wouldn't emerge under normal conditions, so far not a single significant invention has been produced as a result of using these drugs. No classic of literature, no widely hailed set of new ideas about politics, religion, sex, war, science, or industry has emerged after deliberately using mind-expanding drugs. Works of art inspired by the effects of these drugs upon the brain characteristically lack order and coherence.

Present evidence indicates that the experiences fostered by drugs are largely or entirely illusory.

Don't let this chapter blow your mind. Match the slang term with the meaning.

Part I

1. Acid
2. Block
3. Downs
4. Floating
5. Geezer
6. Horn
7. Lemonade
8. Quill
9. Scag
10. Spoon
11. Tracks
12. Ups

A. Barbiturates
B. Scars along the vein after many injections
C. Sniff narcotics
D. 1/16th ounce of heroin
E. A narcotic injection
F. Amphetamines
G. LSD
H. An ounce of hashish
I. Under the influence of drugs
J. Heroin
K. Poor-grade heroin
L. A folded matchbox cover from which narcotics are sniffed through the nose

Part II

1. Bale
2. D.D.
3. Fix
4. Freeze
5. Grass
6. Jag
7. Lid
8. Roach
9. Speedball
10. Sugar
11. Turkey
12. Yen hook

A. A fatal dose
B. Narcotic injection
C. Instrument used in opium smoking
D. Powdered narcotics
E. A pound of marijuana
F. Butt end of a marijuana cigarette
G. Under the influence of amphetamine sulfate
H. Marijuana
I. Cocaine
J. An ounce of marijuana
K. A supposed narcotic capsule filled with a non-narcotic
L. An injection that combines a stimulant and a depressant, often heroin with amphetamine or cocaine

16.　ECONOMICS

The Eiffel Tower, which many Frenchmen regard as one of the ugliest things in the world, is earning real dividends for its stockholders these days. This remarkable tower, which stands in the Champs de Mars, Paris, opposite the Trocadero, rises to a height of 984'. It was built of interlaced ironwork by Alexandre Gustave Eiffel (1832-1923) for the Paris Exposition of 1889 and was for many years the tallest structure in the world. The first visitors were admitted to the tower on May 15, 1889. Eiffel also did the interior engineering for Bartholdi's Statue of Liberty in New York harbor. The people who administer the Eiffel tower have an office at its base. They state that there isn't an industry in France that has a better growth graph than their tower. Admissions are at a record high; suicides, an embarrassment for the tower people, at an all-time low. After more than 350 suicides, including some people who hanged, shot, or poisoned themselves instead of taking the freefall express down, special grillwork and fences were put up. Even then a handful of people managed to crawl through ventilator ducts to jumping-off places.

You don't need to be high to answer the questions in this chapter. Part I is a matchup of economic definitions and terms; Part II identifies some federal laws, and Part III involves defining some abbreviations. If you can't get the right answers, don't head for that ventilator duct.

Part I

1. A plant shut by an employer during a labor dispute to force his terms on employees
2. That part of profits distributed by a corporation to its stockholders in proportion to the amount and kind of their stocks
3. Regular payment plus interest of a sum of money out of funds accumulated in the past
4. Restriction of imports by value of quantity
5. An economy that serves the states and not individuals
6. Paying wages for inessential help or for work done with deliberate slowness
7. Association of rival sellers to exercise control over a market area
8. Carrying uncompleted transactions from one accounting period to the next
9. Stockholder's authorization to another party to vote on his behalf at a company meeting
10. A single buyer
11. Doctrine advocating minimum government guidance of or interference with the economy
12. Claim on the debt of a government or corporation bearing a fixed interest rate
13. A tax on goods of foreign origin
14. Few rival sellers
15. Organized market for trading listed securities or commodities
16. Increase in value of an asset

17. A holding company owning another holding company and so on
18. Rise in the value of money

WORD LIST

A. Accrual	J. Laissez-faire
B. Annuity	K. Lockout
C. Appreciation	L. Mercantilism
D. Bond	M. Monopsonist
E. Cartel	N. Oligopoly
F. Deflation	O. Proxy
G. Dividend	P. Pyramiding
H. Exchange	Q. Quota
I. Featherbedding	R. Tariff

Part II

1. Allows a manufacturer to force all retailers to sell brand-name goods at an agreed price
2. Limited the use of court injunctions against union striking, picketing, and boycotting and outlawed yellow-dog contracts
3. Labor-reform law designed to protect union members from financial abuses by leaders, to promote union democracy, and to restrict organizational picketing and secondary boycott
4. Prohibited price discrimination, buying up shares in a competitor's company, and interlocking directorates
5. Declared every contract, combination, or conspiracy in restraint of trade and any attempt to monopolize illegal
6. Federal law aimed at curbing certain union practices in which a closed shop illegal but a union shop is allowed and that provides for 80-day injunction against strikes endangering the nation's health and safety
7. Established the National Labor Relations Board and requires an employer to bargain with the certified union
8. Prohibits cheaper selling of the same goods under different brands

Law List

A. Sherman Act (1890)	E. Robinson-Patman Act (1936)
B. Clayton Act (1914)	F. Miller-Tydings Act (1937)
C. Norris-LaGuardia Act (1932)	G. Taft-Hartley Act (1947)
D. Wagner Act (1935)	H. Landrum-Griffin Act (1959)

Part III

1. AAA	7. FTC	13. IMF
2. AFL-CIO	8. GATT	14. NLRB
3. CEA	9. GNP	15. NNP
4. EPU	10. IBRD	16. NRA
5. FDIC	11. ICC	17. RFC
6. FHA	12. IFC	18. SEC

17. FAMILIAR PHRASES

What are the origins of the terms "red-letter days," "the jig is up," "make a clean breast of it," "battle royal," and "Adam's apple?"

First things first. Saint's days and other holidays were formerly and usually still are marked in church calendars with red letters. From this custom comes the expression "red-letter day," meaning an especially fortunate or happy one. "Jig" was first heard during Shakespeare's time and was a slang word for "trick," so the phrase simply meant that your trick or deceit had been found out.

"To make a clean breast of it" probably goes back to the ancient custom of branding a sinner on the breast with a symbol appropriate to the evil that he or she had committed. A person who confessed his sins would be one who had "come clean" or "made a clean breast of it." By confessing he had purged himself of sin. The term "battle royal" came into existence when cock fighting was popular. Only two roosters were usually permitted in the ring, but when a king visited the fight, four or more were put in the ring together. Today the expression denotes a fight among several people.

The popular name of the prominence in the front of a man's throat is called the "Adam's apple" from the story in the Old Testament in which the forbidden fruit lodged in Adam's throat.

In this chapter you can hit the jackpot if you can match the phrase with the meaning.

Phrase	Meaning

Part I

1. Knock it off	A. Determine
2. Hard-and-fast	B. Quibble
3. By design	C. Purposely
4. Up in the air	D. Desist
5. Split hairs	E. An agreement
6. Bark at the moon	F. Save
7. With a free hand	G. Lavishly
8. Turn the scales	H. Not settled
9. All along the line	I. Strict
10. Meeting of minds	J. Quickly
11. Like a shot	K. Everywhere
12. Lay aside	L. Make futile protests

Part II

1 Up in arms	A. Close together
2. At issue	B. In dispute
3. Lay it on	C. Gain distinction
4. Cheek to jowl	D. Extremely
5. Rake over the coals	E. Scold
6. Every man jack	F. Exaggerate
7. Bring to book	G. Indignant
8. Win one's spurs	H. Blame for
9. On the rack	I. Apply oneself with vigor
10. Beyond measure	J. In a difficult situation
11. Lay at the door of	K. Force to explain
12. Lay to	L. Everybody

18. FAMOUS ANIMALS

Alfalfa was probably planted in southwestern Asia long before recorded history. Historical records show that man has grown alfalfa for fodder longer than any other forage plant. The Persians took it to Greece when they invaded that country in 490 B.C. Historians believe that alfalfa was introduced from Greece into Italy about the 1st century A.D. and later spread into other parts of Europe. Spanish explorers brought alfalfa to South America during the early 1500s, and European colonists introduced it to North America.

The first recorded attempt to grow alfalfa in the English colonies was made in 1736 in Georgia. The colonists also took the plant to other areas, but it did not become important in North America until about 1850 when seed was brought to California from Chile. The Chilean seed produced excellent crops in the California climate. Alfalfa production gradually spread as far east as the Mississippi River and north to Canada.

This chapter does not deal with food for animals but relates directly to identifying famous animals in history — real or fictional.

Part I

1. Thorne Smith wrote the whimsical story about Topper, who, with his dog, possessed the ability to materialize as a ghost. What was the name of the dog?
2. A horse purchased for $12.50 earned over a million dollars for its cowboy owner, Tom Mix. Name him.
3. Name the horse in the comic strip *Barney Google*
4. A novel by H. Allen Smith was made into a movie in 1951. It was about a cat who inherited a baseball team. The name of the movie was also the name of the cat. Name him.
5. Name the faithful dog of Little Orphan Annie.
6. In the book *Seventeen* by Booth Tarkington Miss Lola Pratt converses with her lap dog in endearing baby talk. Name the dog.
7. The highwayman Dick Turpin was arrested for horse stealing and hanged in York, England in 1739. The celebrated ride to York is immortalized in many books and poems. Name his trusty steed.
8. In the five years from 1947 to 1951 inclusive this horse won over a million dollars, the first million-dollar winner. Name him.
9. In Walt Disney's *Pinocchio* Pinocchio had two pets, a goldfish and a cat. Name them.
10. Dagwood and Blondie in the comic strip had two children and a pet dog, who had a litter of pups. Name their dog.
11. Mythology describes a threeheaded dog of the underworld that constantly guarded the door so that none could enter Hades without permission. Name this dog.

12. Cervantes wrote a famous story about Don Quizote and his servant Sancho Panza. They had a horse that was "so lean, lank, meagre, drooping, sharp-backed and raw-boned as to excite much curiosity and mirth." Name the horse.
13. What was the name of Gene Autry's horse? His footprints are preserved in the cement pavement in front of Grauman's Chinese Theater.
14. In what famous children's story does a cheshire cat appear?
15. A species of cat derives its name from an island in the Irish Sea. What is the name of this cat, which has practically no tail?
16. Name the dog in the Stephen Collins Foster song published in 1853.
17. What mule appeared in many movies with Donald O'Connor?
18. Alexander the Great purchased an unmanageable steed that had never obeyed a rider. The horse willingly obeyed him, and he never rode upon any other horse. After the horse died, Alexander built a city over his grave. Name the horse.
19. What is the name of the cat accidentally sealed in a wall by a murderer?
20. What is the name of the mythological winged horse of the Muses, which sprang from the blood of Medusa?

Part II

1. Which of the following native Australian animals is a placental mammal?
   a. Bandicoot
   b. Dingo
   c. Koala
   d. Wallaby
   e. Wombat
2. Which type of pet or domesticated animal is known by the names Havana, American blue, and Flemish giant?
3. What is the name given to the fur produced from the pelt of the coypu?
4. Which large island is the chief home of the true lemurs?
5. What name is given to the only surviving family of American marsupials?
6. The yak is a native of which country?
7. Man normally has seven bones in his neck; how many does the giraffe have?
8. What is an otary?
9. What kind of animal is a saki?
10. Which small mammal is said to consume its own weight in food about every three hours?
11. What kind of creature is the Indian krait?
12. What is the largest living relative of the hog family?

19.   FOREIGN, ENGLISH, OR AMERICAN?

After a couple of millenia of experimentation with such currency as sceats, stycas, nobles, crosses, crowns, sovereigns, groats, guineas, broads, bonnet pieces, angels, and ryals the British have finally settled down to pounds and pence. The slang terms "bob" and "tanner" are lost, and they have no shilling for the first time in more than 480 years. The shilling, or testoon, was created in 1487 during the reign of King Henry VII.

The fabled ha'penny is as much a part of the English language as Yorkshire pudding. Big as a quarter but worth only half a cent, the British halfpenny ceased to be legal coinage on August 1, 1969. Its demise was part of Britain's approach to D-Day — February 15, 1971 — when the nation converted to decimal currency. The decimal system has a new halfpenny, valued at 1.2 cents. It doesn't buy much more than the old ha'penny. In deciding to do away with the old coin the committee of inquiry concluded that the halfpenny was the least valuable coin ever to have been in common use in the United Kingdom, but it also decided a low-value coin was mandatory in any new money system, mostly for use in retail pricing. The farthing, worth a quarter of a penny, was abolished from the currency system in 1961: "A farthing is only good for a bloody two matches," was a common criticism. The ha'penny had long been an integral part of the price of milk, bread, flour, sugar, potatoes, cigarettes, and gasoline in Britain. To Britons 11½ pence is more alluring than a shilling (12 pence); its American corollary is the $1.99 price tag.

This chapter also concerns similarities. Try your English and give the American counterparts of British terms, the meaning of foreign terms, and the English meaning of foreign expressions.

Part I

1. Way out
2. Salad cream
3. House full
4. Give way
5. Wagon train
6. Supplement
7. Roundabout
8. Lift
9. Biscuits
10. Beef mince

Part II

1. Ad infinitum (Latin)
2. A la carte (French)
3. A la mode (French)
4. Et cetera (Latin)
5. Ex officio (Latin)
6. Finis (Latin)
7. Nom de plume (French)
8. Par excellence (French)
9. Per se (Latin)
10. Tete-a-tete (French)

Part III

1. Affaire d'honneur (French)
2. Bon vivant (French)
3. Coup d'etat (French)
4. Cum grano salis (Latin)
5. Esprit de corps (French)
6. Ex libris (Latin)
7. Faux pas (French)
8. Hoi polloi (Greek)
9. Laissez faire (French)
10. Sans souci (French)
11. Savoir-faire (French)
12. Status quo (Latin)

A. The common people
B. Group spirit
C. Epicure
D. The present situation
E. Without worry
F. An unexpected show of force or authority
G. With a grain of salt
H. A social blunder
I. A duel
J. From (of) the books
K. Noninterference
L. Knowledge of how to act

20. FURNITURE AND HOUSEHOLD ARTICLES

The early North American Indians had no tables, chairs, or stoves. Their only furnishings were beds, which were seats of matting covered with bearskin. These seats extended around the walls of the house and were about 2' from the ground, but the entire household often slept on the floor around the fire. They had no chests or cupboards. From poles near the top of the house hung clothing, weapons, and skins as well as meats, corn, and other food. The soot from the fire made a thick, dirty, black covering on the walls and contents of the house. The household utensils, pots, buckets, and bowls were all made by hand of stone, clay, bark, or skins, depending on what materials were available. The utensils were decorated with pictures of birds, reptiles, animals, or other symbolic designs with paints obtained from minerals or the juices of plants. Drinking cups were often gourds or bison horns, while spoons were made from wood or elk horns. Knives were common and were made of stone. Most tribes made fires by rubbing pieces of flint or sticks of hardwood together.

The tribes that lived by fishing made wooden items such as fish clubbers, fish spears, sealing shafts, whaling harpoons, and raftlike boats. From the fibers they wove nets, and from bones they made hooks. From animal skins they made strips of sinew for their bows and fashioned snowshoes with which they could travel as far as 40 miles a day to catch deer and moose.

The furniture and household articles in this quiz are a little more up-to-date. Match the description with the proper identification in the word list.

1. A kind of elongated couch or seat, usually with a support for the back only at one end
2. A seat or stool without arms or back, so-called from its resemblance to a drum
3. A large basket, especially of wickerwork, in which articles of food or clothing are packed
4. A small, rather shallow dish, usually of earthenware, with straight sides and sometimes ears
5. A water pitcher with a wide mouth or spout
6. A long seat or bench, generally of wood, with a high back and often arms, accommodating several persons
7. An ornamental glass bottle for liquors, adapted for use at the table
8. An article of furniture with a set of shelves for holding bric-a-brac, ornaments, books, and so on
9. A basket with a wicker hood over one end, used as a child's cradle
10. A metal case or box for tea, coffee, spices, and so on
11. A container to keep cigars moist
12. A pan for holding burning coals
13. A cushioned seat without a back, resembling a Turkish divan
14. A small, stuffed cushion or footstool for kneeling on in church
15. A tall, commodious chest of drawers standing on high legs
16. A Russian urn, commonly of copper, to hold boiling water for making tea

WORD LIST

A. Brazier	E. Decanter	I. Hautboy	M. Samovar
B. Bassinet	F. Ewer	J. Humidor	N. Settle
C. Canister	G. Hamper	K. Porringer	O. Taboret
D. Chaise lounge	H. Hassock	L. Ottoman	P. Whatnot

21. HOMONYMS

A prune is a dried plum and plums that are especially well suited to the drying process are known as prune plums. They have such firm flesh and such a high sugar content that they can be dried without losing much of their original plumpness and flavor. There are four leading varieties of prune plums in the United States. The French plum, brought to California in 1856 by Louis Pellier, is the chief type grown in this country. The others are the imperial, sugar, and sergeant prune plums. Prune plums are harvested in August. The trees require a warm climate and much sun. They become profitable at eight years of age. When the plums are fully tree-ripened, they fall and are removed in baskets for drying.

Although prunes and plums are the same, they are not pronounced and spelled in the same way. On the other hand, a homonym is a word with the same pronunciation as another but differing from it in origin, meaning, and often in spelling. In this quiz for each example there are three meanings. The answers are pronounced similarly but spelled differently: for example, corresponding to the meanings passage, island, and I will are the words aisle, isle, and I'll.

1.	a. Yes	b. Organ of sight	c. Myself
2.	a. Come into life	b. A limit	c. Carried
3.	a. Weight	b. Mark	c. Vegetable
4.	a. Coin	b. Caused to go	c. Odor
5.	a. Summons	b. Situation	c. View
6.	a. Moisture	b. To perform	c. Own
7.	a. Sheep	b. Trees	c. To employ
8.	a. Pleased	b. Temple	c. Pretend
9.	a. Animal	b. Not old	c. Understood
10.	a. Image	b. Unemployed	c. Poem
11.	a. Rogue	b. Artless	c. Center
12.	a. Falsifier	b. Musical instrument	c. One who lies down
13.	a. Denoting pain	b. Surprise	c. Indebted
14.	a. Mineral	b. Over	c. Paddle
15.	a. A couple	b. To peel	c. A fruit
16.	a. The top	b. Grudge	c. To peep
17.	a. Water	b. Rule	c. Bridle
18.	a. To lift	b. Sunbeams	c. To demolish
19.	a. Correct	b. Ceremony	c. To form letters
10.	a. Color	b. Impelled by oars	c. River
21.	a. Water	b. Looks	c. Take hold of
22.	a. Valley	b. A fee	c. To cover
23.	a. Blood vessel	b. Weathercock	c. Proud
24.	a. Road	b. Watery part of milk	c. To balance
25.	a. To impair by use	b. Merchandise	c. In which place

22. INVENTOR AND INVENTION

Let's take a look at how the cable cars of San Francisco work. In principle nothing is simpler than to use a rope to pull a vehicle up a hill, but in practice the cable car and its attendant machinery are a miracle of inventiveness. The connection between the car and the cable is an ingenious and most necessary device called a grip. The car moves when the gripman pulls back on the operating lever, closing a pincerlike hold on the endless cable that is kept continuously in motion by electric motors in the carhouse. The grip itself is a semicylinder about 1' long and made of two parts that rehinge and close over each side of the cable like a vise. When the operator pulls back on the griplever, a heavy metal plate descends against this cylinder, forcing the two curved hinges, or grip dies, to close around the cable. Two rollers, one on each side of the hinges, guide them over the cable. As the grip lever is pulled, pressure is put on the rope and the car is slowly put into motion, the tar on the cable acting as a lubricant to permit a smooth start and to reduce friction.

That's how it starts, but how does it stop? There are four separate braking devices on each car, and both the gripman and the conductor share responsibilities for this phase of the operation. To operate the wheel brake, the gripman depresses a foot lever that activates a metal shoe, which clamps down on the front wheels. The conductor also turns a hand lever on the rear platform to operate the rear truck-wheel brake when descending very steep grades. The cable itself is actually a type of brake, for when it is held tight by the grip, a descending car cannot go faster than its steady nine miles per hour. The track brakes are wooden blocks about 2' long, 2" deep, and 3" wide, which fit between the two wheels on one or both trucks of the front and rear chassis. The blocks, or track shoes, are in position over each rail and operated by the gripman, using a large hand lever on the front end of the car. The blocks clamp down directly on the rail, almost lifting the car up slightly, and are quite effective as brakes. The blocks are cut from soft, clear pine and last about four days during summer months and two days during winter months when the wood soaks up moisture and wears out more rapidly. The emergency or slot brake is used only as a last resort. When the red-handled hot-line lever is pulled, it causes a guillotinelike, tapered piece of metal 18" long and 1" thick to instantly penetrate the cable slot until it is wedged tight by pressure, friction, and heat. It not only stops the car instantaneously but usually requires the services of a welding crew to burn it off.

Don't put on the brakes to match the invention or the inventor in this quiz.

Invention | **Inventor**

Part I

Invention	Inventor
1. Rigid airship (1900)	A. James Hargreaves
2. Balloon (1783)	B. Alfred B. Nobel
3. Electric battery (1800)	C. Ferdinand von Zeppelin
4. Carburetor (1892)	D. Joseph Aspdin
5. Portland cement (1824)	E. Hans Lippershey
6. Dynamite (1866)	F. J. M. and J. E. Montgolfier
7. Miner's lamp (1815)	G. Gottlieb Daimler
8. Radar (1935)	H. Robert A. Watson-Watt
9. Spinning machine (1764)	I. Humphry Davy
10. Telescope (1608)	J. Allessandro Volta

Part II

Invention	Inventor
1. Air brake (1869)	A. Glenn H. Curtis
2. Bifocal lens (1780)	B. Benjamin Franklin
3. Cash register (1879)	C. Hamilton E. Smith
4. Cylinder lock (1865)	D. Ottmar Mergenthaler
5. Electric vacuum cleaner (1907)	E. George Westinghouse
6. Hydroplane (1911)	F. Linus Yale, Jr.
7. Linotype (1884)	G. Edgar T. Holmes
8. Safety pin (1849)	H. Walter Hunt
9. Switchboard (1877)	I. James M. Spangler
10. Washing machine (1858)	J. James Ritty

Part III

Invention	Inventor
1. Air conditioning (1911)	A. John B. Meyenberg
2. Bottle-making machine (1903)	B. Michael Owens
3. Color photography (1881)	C. Thomas A. Edison
4. Electric stove (1896)	D. Peter C. Hewitt
5. Evaporated milk (1880)	E. Willis H. Carrier
6. Mercury-vapor lamp (1901)	F. Whitcomb L. Judson
7. Machine gun (1862)	G. Lee De Forest
8. Stock ticker (1870)	H. Frederic E. Ives
9. Triode vacuum tube (1906)	I. Richard J. Gatling
10. Zipper (1893)	J. William S. Hadaway, Jr.

23. LANDMARKS OF SCIENCE

In ancient Rome people sacrificed a red dog to Robigus, the rust god, for they thought that there was some connection between the dog star and epidemics of a rusty-red blight that often appeared on growing wheat and barley. The ancient Greeks made supplications to the corn goddess so that evil might be averted, and when the harvest was safely gathered in, they paid tribute with offerings of grain.

Not until the invention of the microscope in the 17th century was man provided with the means of determining the causes of plant diseases. Early investigators gazed into their microscopes and saw minute living organisms. What they discovered were tiny plants, bacteria, and fungi.

The theory of spontaneous generation of disease was finally put to rest by the French chemist, physician, and bacteriologist Louis Pasteur. His experiments showed that fermentation and putrefaction were the result of natural causes, the activities of microorganisms. Two new sciences were developed: bacteriology, the study of bacteria; and mycology, the study of fungi. The germ theory of disease was securely established, and the road was clear to the conquest of many diseases that plagued mankind, his livestock, and his crops.

In 1892 the Russian scientist Ivanowski discovered another causal agent of disease in addition to parasitic fungi and bacteria. He found that the sap of diseased tobacco plants with a peculiar mosaic appearance was infectious to healthy plants. It was still infectious after it had been passed through filters that held back bacteria and other known microorganisms. Other diseases of a somewhat similar nature were later discovered, and it was shown that this kind of ailment was not due to microscopic fungi or bacteria but to an infection principle or virus. Today, of course, many such maladies are known, and there seems to be no limit to their diversity, for they plague almost every form of life. Man is affected with yellow fever, typhus, mumps, smallpox, and measles; cattle suffer from foot-and-mouth disease; and potatoes, from leaf roll and mosaic.

Don't get feverish if you can't match the landmark of science with the person associated with it in this chapter.

1. Publication of *De re metallica,* establishing the science of mineralogy (1556)
2. First cylindrical-projection map, establishing map making (1559)
3. Discovery of the laws of motion concerning falling bodies, the pendulum, and the inclined plane (1589-92)
4. Publication of *De magnete,* the basis for future work on magnetism and electricity (1600)
5. Discovery of the three fundamental laws of planetary motion (1609-19)
6. Invention of logarithms, the most powerful method of arithmetical calculation (1614)
7. Formulation of analytic geometry (1619)
8. Publication of *Novum Organum,* elucidating the first formal theory of inductive logic (1620)
9. Proof that air has weight; invention of the barometer (1643)
10. Discovery of the law governing the relation between pressure and volume of a gas (1662)
11. Publication of *Philosophiae naturalis principia mathematica,* establishing the laws of gravitation and the universal laws of motion (1687)
12. Discovery of electromagnetism (1820)
13. Founding of the science of oceanography (1855)
14. Formulation of the fundamental laws of genetics (1865)
15. Formulation of the periodic law and periodic table of elements (1869)
16. Discovery of radioactivity in uranium (1896)
17. Postulation of the quantum theory (1900)
18. Publication of *Conditioned Reflexes* (1926)
19. First successful firing of the liquid fuel rocket (1926)
20. Neutron bombardment of uranium, leading to the production of transuranium elements (1934)

Writer or Discoverer

A. Antoine H. Becquerel
B. Robert H. Goddard
C. Isaac Newton
D. John Napier
E. Hans Christian Oersted
F. Gerhard Kremer (Mercator)
G. Rene Descartes
H. Matthew F. Maury
I. Max Planck
J. Francis Bacon

K. Georg Bauer (Agricola)
L. Dmitri I. Mendeleev
M. Enrico Fermi
N. Gregor J. Mendel
O. Robert Boyle
P. Galileo Galilei
Q. William Gilbert (or Gylberde)
R. Ivan Petrovich Pavlov
S. Evangelista Torricelli
T. Johannes Kepler

24. MATCH YOUR PHOBIAS

It is widely believed that rattlesnakes always rattle before they strike, that they can't climb over a hair rope or a wall of cactus, and that whiskey is helpful in treating snakebite. As it happens, these and many other ideas about rattlesnakes are untrue.

Rattlesnakes can be encountered at almost any altitude. Most people don't expect to find them at altitudes over 6,000', but in the southwestern United States they have been encountered as high as the 11,000' level, and in Mexico up to 14,000'. In most parts of the country rattlesnakes hibernate in dens in the winter, but they are generally in the open from March or April to October or December, depending on local climate and weather conditions.

The most distinctive feature of the rattlesnake is its rattle, which it vibrates when it is disturbed or annoyed. The actual sound is a kind of toneless buzz or hiss, which is sometimes confused with the sound made by the cicada. Although it was once supposed that these snakes acquired one new rattle each year, it has now been established that they get a new one each time that they shed their skins, which may be from one to four times a year, depending on age, species, and climate.

There are some 30 different kinds of rattlesnakes in the United States, and they vary greatly in size, markings, and coloration. Neither large nor small rattlesnakes have the ability to travel rapidly over the ground, which is so often attributed to them in legend. Far from being able to keep up with a galloping horse, they can't even match the speed of a man in any kind of a hurry. The rattler's strike, on the other hand, is a rapid motion, so fast that the reptile's head cannot be followed by the human eye. At the end of the strike the rattler's mouth is wide open, with the fangs in the upper jaw swung forward to pierce whatever is struck.

Judged purely on mortality statistics, rattlesnakes offer no outstanding hazard to man. The number of people killed in the United States every year does not exceed 30 or 35, which is less than the number killed annually by lightning. At the same time rattlers pose a constant threat to anyone working or vacationing in rural or wilderness areas, and more knowledge about their habits and actions might reduce the number of painful and sometimes fatal bites that are suffered each year.

If you don't have a phobia about answering questions about phobias, then try to match the phobias with their definition.

Fear of   **Phobia**

Part I

1. Darkness	A. Aelurophobia
2. Blushing	B. Aichmaphobia
3. Sharp instruments	C. Carcinomaphobia
4. Tapeworms	D. Cenophobia
5. Water	E. Ereuthrophobia
6. Cats	F. Hydrophobia
7. Number 13	G. Mysophobia
8. Thunder	H. Nyctophobia
9. Cancer	I. Ophidiophobia
10. Dirt or contamination	J. Pyrophobia
11. Large halls or auditoriums	K. Teniophobia
12. Snakes	L. Tontriphobia
13. Fire	M. Triakaidekaphobia

Part II

1. Dogs	A. Agoraphobia
2. Open fields, parks, or squares	B. Bacillophobia
3. Illness	C. Catagelphobia
4. Burial alive	D. Cynophobia
5. Foreigners or foreign practices	E. Gynephobia
6. Crowds	F. Kaintophobia
7. Animals or a particular species of animal	G. Nosophobia
8. Women	H. Ochlophobia
9. Small, enclosed spaces	I. Claustrophobia
10. Death	J. Taphephobia
11. Change	K. Thanatophobia
12. Infection by microbes	L. Xenophobia
13. Ridicule	M. Zoophobia

25. MATHEMATICAL TERMS

The Greek word for "angle" is *gonia,* and for "much" is *polys.* A closed figure containing a number of angles is therefore a polygon. The particular variety of polygon is named after Greek numbers: a five-angled figure is a pentagon — *pente* is "five"; an eight-angled figure is an octagon — *okto* is "eight"; and a six-angled figure is a hexagon — *hes* is "six". On this system a four-angled figure ought to be a tetragon, and a three-angled one a trigon. Although these two terms are found in the dictionary, they are practically never used. The Latin equivalents are used instead: a four-angled figure is a quadrangle, or, even more commonly, a quadrilateral — *quattuor* is Latin for "four" — and a three-angled figure is a triangle — *tres* is Latin for "three".

A polygon with four equal sides is equilateral, from the Latin *aequus,* meaning "equal," and *latus,* meaning "side". The only equilateral polygon with a special name of its own is the equilateral quadrangle, which is a square if all the angles are right angles or a rhombus if they are not. A triangle with three equal sides is an equilateral triangle; one with only two sides equal is an isosceles triangle. The word "isosceles" is derived from the image of a man's two legs standing apart, which forms an isosceles triangle with the ground.

You certainly won't be considered a square if you can match the definitions with the correct words in both parts of this quiz.

Part I

1. The line that a curve approaches indefinitely without meeting it in any finite distance
2. The process by which any number or expression is broken into its component parts when the parts are multiplied together
3. The perpendicular line segment from the center of a regular polygon to a side
4. The Latin word for makeweight given to the positive fractional part of a logarithm
5. The conic section made by a plane parallel to a generating line of a cone
6. A point at which a tangent crosses a curve
7. An assumption upon which a logical argument is based
8. Any standardized procedure for solving a particular type of problem
9. The most frequently occurring value in a series of measurements or observations
10. The conic section made by a plane that cuts only one nappe of a cone to produce a continuous curve
11. A proposition that is proved in order to prove another proposition
12. Identical in position

WORD LIST

A. Algorithm
B. Apothem
C. Asymptote
D. Coincident
E. Ellipse
F. Factorization
G. Inflexion
H. Lemma
I. Mantissa
J. Mode
K. Parabola
L. Postulate

Part II

1. The locus in a plane of a point on the circumference of a circle, which rolls without slipping on the outside of a fixed circle
2. The branch of arithmetic that deals with the measurement of geometrical shapes and the consequent calculations to determine length, area, and volume
3. Having at least two sides of equal length
4. The portion of a plane bounded by the circumferences of two concentric circles in the plane
5. The conic section made by a plane that cuts both nappes of a cone
6. A horizontal line used to separate the numerator from the denominator in a common fraction
7. Neither parallel nor perpendicular to a given direction
8. The curve assumed by a uniform, flexible, heavy chain or cable hanging freely from its extremities
9. The exponent that indicates the power to which a number must be raised to produce a given number
10. The length of a closed curve
11. A double point on a curve at which the tangents are real and distinct
12. Part of a curve as distinct from the whole

WORD LIST

A. Annulus
B. Arc
C. Catenary
D. Crunode
E. Epicycloid
F. Hyperbola

G. Isosceles
H. Logarithm
I. Mensuration
J. Oblique
K. Perimeter
L. Vinvulum

26. MEDICAL AILMENTS

What makes our teeth chatter? Why do some of us have freckles? What causes a lump in a person's throat?

When a person is cold, he is apt to have a spasm of shivering over which his brain does not seem to have any control. The spasm causes the muscles of the jaw to contract very quickly, and as soon as they are extracted, they let the jaw fall again of its own weight. This spasm-and-relaxation pattern, occurring many times in rapid succession, causes the teeth to chatter. There are two kinds of spasms, clonic and tonic. In the former the muscles contract and relax alternately in very quick succession, producing an appearance of agitation. In the latter the muscles contract in a steady, uniform manner and remain contracted for a comparatively long time.

Some people have freckles while others do not because all skins are not alike, just as all eyes are not the same color. People with certain kinds of skin freckle more quickly with exposure to the sun. The action of the sun causes small parts of the second layer of skin to give out a yellow or yellowish brown substance. Freckles are most common in persons with fair complexion and hair. In some cases freckles are permanent, but they usually disappear with cold weather.

When someone eats something, it passes into his throat after he has chewed it, and a 9" or 10" series of rings passes or squeezes it from one set of muscle rings to the next. These muscle rings can move the food both up and down: if something is eaten that causes vomiting, the muscles work backwards and force the matter from the stomach. When one is frightened, a hollow sensation is felt in the stomach, and, the throat muscles work upward, pressing against the windpipe and causing one to feel as if there was a lump.

There's no need to get a lump in your throat while trying this quiz. Match the descriptions with the ailments in each part.

Part I

1. Protrusion of a portion of an organ or tissue through an abnormal body opening
2. A marked lateral curvature of the normally straight vertical spine
3. Chronic, occasionally acute, recurrent skin disease of unknown cause, characterized by thickened red skin patches that are covered with whitish, shiny scales
4. Disease characterized by sudden and brief convulsions
5. Hereditary or acquired sugar-utilization deficiency
6. Inflammation of the tubular passages leading to the lung cavities
7. Excessive accumulation of water and salt in the tissue spaces caused by kidney or heart disease or by local circulatory impairment stemming from inflammation, trauma, or neoplasm
8. Condition caused by inflammation of a vein wall, resulting in the formation of a blood clot inside its cavity
9. A disease caused by niacin deficiency, characterized by skin, alimentary-tract, and nervous-system disturbances
10. Inflammation of the enveloping membranes of the brain or spinal cord, caused by virus, bacteria, yeasts, fungi, or protozoa
11. Brief attack of acute and severe shooting pain along one or more peripheral nerves, usually without clear cause
12. Eye disease characterized by an increase in internal pressure
13. An inherited disease of the external-secretion glands that affects the pancreas, respiratory tract, and sweat glands and usually is manifested in infancy
14. Chronic liver ailment characterized by an increase in fibrous support tissue, which results in a progressive destruction of liver cells and impairment of the organ's functions
15. Generalized thickening, loss of elasticity, and hardening of the body's small and medium-size arteries
16. Inflammation of the heart muscle associated with or caused by a number of infectious diseases, toxic chemicals, drugs, and traumatic agents

WORD LIST

A. Arteriosclerosis	G. Epilepsy	M. Pellagra
B. Bronchitis	H. Glaucoma	N. Phlebitis
C. Cirrhosis	I. Hernia	O. Psoriasis
D. Cystic fibrosis	J. Meningitis	P. Sooliosis
E Diabetes	K. Myocarditis	
F. Edema	L. Neuralgia	

Part II

1. A chronic and slowly progressive disease of unknown cause that is characterized by patches of fibrous-tissue degeneration in the brain and spinal cord and itself causes various symptoms in the nervous system
2. Accumulation of air or gas in the pleural cavity (between the chest wall and the lung), resulting in lung collapse
3. Acute or chronic inflammation of the stomach lining
4. Disease characterized by repeated attacks of breath shortness, wheezing, coughing, and choking due to a spasmodic narrowing of the small bronchi
5. Lung disease characterized by overdistension of the chest and destruction of the walls separating the lung air sacs
6. Acute or chronic inflammation of the urinary bladder, caused by infection or irritation from foreign bodies or chemicals
7. A usually chronic condition marked by muscular rigidity, immobile facial features, excessive salivation, and tremor
8. An occupational disease causing fibrosis of the lungs, usually chronic and resulting from inhalation of stone, flint, or sand dust
9. Inflammatory acute or chronic disease of the kidneys, which usually follows some form of infection or toxic chemical poisoning and impairs renal function, causing headache, dropsy, elevated blood pressure, and albumin in the urine
10. A disease of infants and young children caused by vitamin-D deficiency
11. Disease characterized by elevated blood pressure, resulting from the functional or pathological narrowing of the peripheral small arteries
12. Acute or chronic inflammation of the serous membrane lining the abdominal walls and covering the contained viscerae, with symptoms such as abdominal pain and tenderness, nausea, vomiting, moderate fever, and constipation
13. Liver inflammation caused by infection or toxics and characterized by jaundice
14. Inflammatory skin disease that produces a great variety of lesions, such as vesicles, thickening of skin, water discharge, scales, and crusts, as well as itching and burning sensations
15. Acute or chronic inflammation of the conjunctiva — the delicate transparent membrane lining the eyelids and covering the exposed surface of the eyeball
16. Opacity of the normally transparent eye lens

WORD LIST

A. Asthma
B. Cataract
C. Conjunctivitis
D. Cystitis
E. Eczema
F. Emphysema

G. Gastritis
H. Hepatitis
I. Hypertension
J. Multiple sclerosis
K. Nephritis

L. Parkinsonism
M. Peritonitis
N. Pneumothorax
O. Rickets
P. Silicosis

27. MATCH THE -OLOGIES

The suffix "logy" is derived from the Greek *lego*, "to speak," or *logos*, "discourse." The earliest branch of science that was given this suffix was anthropology in 1593. Since the end of the 18th century the suffix has become widespread.

In fact, this quiz is concerned with only 20 from a list of hundreds. If you succeed in matching the study to the correct-ology, you must be some kind of -ologist yourself.

Study **-Ology**

Part I

Study	-Ology
1. Ants	A. Auxology
2. Caves	B. Cartology
3. Deserts	C. Dermatology
4. Faith	D. Entomology
5. Growth	E. Eremology
6. Insects	F. Myrmecology
7. Maps	G. Pistology
8. Nutrition	H. Speleology
9. Poisons	I. Threpsology
10. Skin	J. Toxicology

Part II

Study	-Ology
1. Birds	A. Dendrology
2. Clouds	B. Iatrology
3. Eggs	C. Necrology
4. Fossils	D. Nephology
5. Hair	E. Nomology
6. Law	F. Oology
7. Medicine	G. Ornithology
8. Obituaries	H. Oryctology
9. Rivers	I. Potamology
10. Trees	J. Trichology

28. NICKNAMES OF AMERICAN STATESMEN

How did the expression "okay" originate? To dispel two myths surrounding the term, it did not originate as an abbreviation of "orl kerrect" from the pen of the semiliterate clerk who later became President Andrew Jackson. Jackson was never that close to illiteracy; he was never a clerk of the court where the incident was supposed to have occurred — he was prosecutor — and the initials involved were actually "O.R." for "order recorded," not "OK".

Another favorite legend is that the correct spelling is "okeh," which originated in the Choctaw Indian language. This, too, is probably nonsense.

"Okay" probably originated with the Democratic O.K. Club, a group that supported the candidacy of Martin Van Buren for a second term in 1840. Van Buren was the eighth president of the United States. He was born in the Hudson River Valley of New York State in the little town of Kinderhook, an ancient place that had been settled in early Dutch days. He was often called the Kinderhook Fox, though his admirers preferred Sage of Kinderhook. The Democratic Old Kinderhook Club became the Democratic O.K. Club, and "OK" became a password for its members, later passing into general use as an expression of approval.

This chapter will be okay all the way if you correctly match the nicknames to the American statesmen.

Part I

1. Father of the Constitution
2. The Rail Splitter
3. Little Magician and Wizard of Kinderhook
4. Sage of Monticello
5. Old Rough-and-Ready
6. Hero of Appomattox
7. Young Hickory
8. Old Hickory
9. Father of His Country
10. Colossus of Debate
11. Veto Mayor
12. Old Public Functionary
13. Cowboy President

Name List

A. John Adams
B. James Buchanan
C. Grover Cleveland
D. Ulysses S. Grant
E. Andrew Jackson
F. Thomas Jefferson
G. Abraham Lincoln
H. James Madison
I. James K. Polk
J. Theodore Roosevelt
K. Zachary Taylor
L. Martin Van Buren
M. George Washington

Part II

1, Pathfinder
2. Expounder of the Constitution
3. Hell 'n' Maria
4. Me Too
5. Sage of Greystone
6. Battling Bob
7. Father of the Revolution and American Cato
8. Old White Hat
9. Great Pacificator
10. Boy Orator
11. Little Giant
12. Kingfish
13. Old Bullion
14. Plumed Knight and Magnetic Statesman

Name List

A. Samuel Adams
B. Senator Thomas H. Benton of Missouri
C. James G. Blaine
D. William Jennings Bryan
E. Henry Clay
F. Vice President Charles G. Dawes
G. Stephen A. Douglas
H. John C. Fremont
I. Horace Greeley
J. R.M. LaFollette (the Elder)
K. Senator Huey P. Long of Louisiana
L. Senator Thomas C. Platt of New York
M. Samuel J. Tilden
N. Daniel Webster

29. MORE OR LESS

Because of the variations in the days on which dates fall and in the date of Easter a person born on Easter Sunday may face a long wait until his birthdate and Easter Sunday coincide again. A child born on Easter Sunday, 1962 — April 22 — will have an Easter Sunday birthday in 1973 and 1984 but not again in this century. An Easter Sunday baby of 1963 — April 14 — will have Easter Sunday anniversaries in 1968 and 1974. Easter Sunday can fall no earlier than March 22 and no later than April 25. The earliest it will fall in the balance of this century is March 26 in the years 1978 and 1989. The latest will be April 23 in 2000. It will arrive on April 24 in 2011 and April 25 in 2038.

Easter falls on the first Sunday after the Paschal full moon. The Paschal full moon does not necessarily coincide with the astronomical full moon. The 14th day of the Paschal moon falls on or after the vernal equinox, which is arbitrarily designated as March 21 for Easter computations. The Paschal full moon sometimes falls on a Sunday, in which case, Easter falls on the following Sunday.   This quiz is concerned with other things that are either more or less something compared with similar things.

Which is:

1. Farther north — Caribou, Maine or Penasse, Minnesota?
2. Older — the Neanderthal or the Cro-Magnon period?
3. Pinker — a talisman rose or a cabbage rose?
4. More durable — marble or granite?
5. More feathery — cirrus or cumulus clouds?
6. More valuable — the Hope or the Koh-i-Nor diamond?
7. Smaller in area — Illinois or Idaho?
8. Harder — bituminous coal or anthracite coal?
9. More ornamental — a Corinthian column or a Doric column?
10. More — MCM or DCV?
11. More fattening — heavy whipping cream or peanut butter?
12. Faster — light waves or sound waves?
13. Heavier — iron or lead?
14. More destructive — a monsoon or a typhoon?
15. More negotiable — a Joe Miller or an Annie Oakley?
16. Larger — the earth or Mars?

30. NOBEL PRIZE WINNERS

Alfred Bernhard Nobel, born in Stockholm in 1833, was a Swedish manufacturer, inventor, and philanthropist. He was educated in St. Petersburg and the United States, where he studied mechanical engineering. He invented dynamite in 1866 and ballistite, one of the first smokeless powders, in 1888. He is also credited with the invention of artificial gutta-percha and over 100 other patented items. His main wealth came through the manufacture of dynamite and other explosives in various parts of the world, and before his death in 1896 he bequeathed a fund of $9,200,000 to establish the Nobel prizes. They were awarded annually in each of five categories to a person or persons "who shall have conferred the greatest benefit on mankind." The awards were to be made without regard to nationality. The first awards were given in 1901, and the five categories were physics, physiology and medicine, chemistry, literature, and peace. On May 15, 1968 it was announced that a sixth category — economic sciences — had been established with funds from the Swedish Riksbank and was to be first awarded by the Royal Swedish Academy of Sciences in 1969.

You only have to worry about the first five categories in this quiz. The first part lists Americans, and the second all other nationalities. Identify the category in which they won their prize: physics, physiology and medicine, chemistry, literature, or peace.

Part I

1. Robert S. Mulliken (1966)
2. Carl D. Anderson (1936)
3. Ralph J. Bunche (1950)
4. Donald A. Glaser (1960)
5. Willard F. Libby (1960)
6. Arthur Kornberg (1959)
7. Robert B. Woodward (1965)
8. Ernest O. Lawrence (1939)
9. Eugene O'Neill (1936)
10. Norman E. Borlaug (1970)
11. Willis E. Lamb, Jr. (1935)
12. Sinclair Lewis (1930)
13. Martin Luther King, Jr. (1964)
14. Arthur D. Hershey (1969)
15. Robert A. Millikan (1923)

Part II

1. Pierre Curie (1903)
2. Dorothy C. Hodgkin (1964)
3. Sir Winston Churchill (1953)
4. Dag Hammarskjold (1961)
5. Anatole France (1921)
6. Alfred Kastler (1966)
7. Albert Schweitzer (1952)
8. Jaroslav Heyrovsky (1959)
9. Ivan P. Pavlov (1904)
10. Wilhelm C. Roentgen (1901)
11. Albert Camus (1957)
12. Lester B. Pearson (1957)
13. John Galsworthy (1932)
14. Paul H. Muller (1948)
15. Salvatore Quasimodo (1959)

31. A NUMBER OF THINGS

The standard-time-zone system is based on the division of the world into 24 zones, each of 15 degrees longitude. The zero time zone is centered at the Greenwich meridian, with longitudes 7½ degrees W. and 7¼ degrees E. as its western and eastern limits, and there is no difference in the standard time of this zone and Greenwich Mean Time. The 12th time zone is divided by the 180th meridian, sometimes known as the International Date Line. This is a hypothetical line that was fixed by international agreement as the place at which the calendar date changes by one day. Crossing the International Date Line to the west, the date is advanced one day; crossing to the east, the date is moved back one day.

This quiz is also concerned with numbers. Take your time in trying to answer the questions.

1. Name the three vice presidents who served under Franklin D. Roosevelt.
2. Name the seven deadly sins.
3. Who is supposed to have sat 49 days under a bo tree?
4. Name the Four Horsemen of the Apocalypse.
5. Name the six wives of Henry VIII of England.
6. Euclid proved that there are infinitely many prime numbers. How many of these are even?
7. Caesar said, "All Gaul is divided into three parts." Name them.
8. On June 5, 1942 the United States declared war on three countries. Name them.
9. Name the seven cardinal virtues.
10. Name the men who were known as The Big Four of the 1919 Paris Peace Conference.
11. Which three countries formed a league known as the Holy Alliance in 1815?
12. How many named bones are there in the adult human body?
    a. 117   b. 206   c. 430   d. 604
13. How many tides occur in 24 hours?
14. In 1841 the United States had three presidents. Name them.
15. How many states in the United States must approve an amendment to the Constitution in order that it be adopted?
16. Identify the following Crusades:
    a. The Crusade that got away and conquered Christian Constantinople
    b. The Crusade preached by Urban II and led by Raymond of Toulouse and Godfrey of Bouillon
    c. The Crusade in which Frederick Barbarossa, Philip Augustus, and Richard the Lion-Hearted took part
17. In 1914 there were only two independent countries in Africa. Name them.
18. What is absolute zero to the nearest whole number on the Centigrade scale?
19. Name the four distinct tastes that the human tongue can identify.
20. Name the Big Three who concluded the Potsdam conference.

32. OCCULT AND MYSTICAL LANGUAGE

The basic concepts of astrology date back over 5,000 years. Astrologists say that the position of the sun, moon, and planets at the time of your birth affects your entire life. These solar bodies move at different speeds, and their relationship constantly changes. Astrologers plot their position at the exact hour, day, and year in which you were born on a birth chart, or horoscope. Using this chart and referring to manuals based on ancient beliefs and manuscripts, they translate these cosmic influences in terms of your potential characteristics, latent talents, and natural tendencies — to cast a guide for your future life as written in the stars.

Every person is born under a Zodiac sign. The Zodiac is a kind of cosmic calendar — a giant imaginary circle encompassing what seems to be the sun's yearly path around earth. Its 12 parts are named for ancient star constellations: each has a characteristic symbol, or sign. The part in which the sun is located when you are born denotes your sign. Your Zodiac sun sign is the strongest single influence, and basic character is often read by this sign alone.

No matter when you were born, you have an equal chance to answer the following questions correctly by matching the definitions against the correct word in the list.

1. A noisy, malicious, discarnate spirit that causes inexplicable disturbances and moves material objects
2. A deck of playing cards based on a system of occult symbols arranged in a pattern
3. The mysterious substance that streams forth from the bodies of mediums
4. The ability to see things and events regardless of distance
5. The attempt by act or intent to gain the favor of a god, demon, or spirit and expiate one's guilt and its divine displeasure
6. A male witch
7. The study of supernormal abilities and phenomena
8. The faculty or practice of moving material objects by thought
9. Divination by writing in ashes
10. A society or club of witches
11. The interpretation of dreams
12. The art of discovering hidden objects with the aid of a rod or twig
13. A medium
14. A person able to foretell future events
15. The raising of images of the dead and the practice of infusing life into the unconscious elementaries of the dead and using them for evil ends
16. Transmission of thoughts from one mind to another

WORD LIST

A. Clairvoyance	E. Oneiroscopy	I. Psychic	M. Telekinesis
B. Coven	F. Parapsychology	J. Rhabdomancy	N. Telepathy
C. Ectoplasm	G. Poltergeist	K. Soothsayer	O. Tephromancy
D. Necromancy	H. Propitiation	L. Tarot	P. Warlock

33. ORIGINS OF NAMES

What is the origin of the expressions "stool pigeon," "taken down a peg," "to be blacklisted," "take a back seat," and "French leave?"

It was an old custom of hunters to fasten a captive wild pigeon to a stool and to move the bird up and down from a place of concealment in order to attract passing flocks of birds. Thus, "stool pigeon" came to mean a decoy or police spy.

The next saying comes from the British Navy. The flag used to be raised or lowered according to the prominence of visitors. The line was fastened by pegs, giving rise to the expression "taken down a peg."

"To be blacklisted" goes back to King Charles II of England, who listed in a black book the 56 men who had sentenced his father, Charles I, to death. They were all subsequently executed.

The fourth expression started in England. Members of Parliament belonging to the majority party got the front seats, and those in the minority were left with the rear seats in the House of Commons and hence had to "take a back seat."

Most authorities believe that the last term, "French leave," can be traced to the 18th-century French custom of withdrawing from crowded assemblies without taking leave of the host and hostess. Another possible explanation is that the word "French" is a corruption of the word *frank*, meaning "free."

The exact origin of some first names is lost in time, but most can be traced not only as to nationality but also as to general meaning. In this quiz match the girls' and boys' names in each part with their origin and meaning.

Part I

1. A friendly elf or brownie (Scandinavian)	A. Amanda
2. Victorious one (Sanskrit)	B. Bonita
3. Woodlark, purity (Old Welsh)	C. Cleo
4. Leaping water (Choctaw Indian)	D. Dinah
5. Thought (French)	E. Enid
6. Estate or home ruler (Old French)	F. Fernanda
7. Pretty (Spanish)	G. Giselle
8. Lady or mistress (Aramaic)	H. Harriet
9. World-daring (Gothic)	I. Ilka
10. Worthy of love (Latin)	J. Jayne
11. Pledge, hostage (Old German)	K. Keely
12. Sky (Hawaiian)	L. Lani
13. Holy one (Old Norse)	M. Martha
14. Brilliant one (Persian)	N. Nissa
15. First-born daughter (Sioux Indian)	O. Olga
16. Glory, fame (Greek)	P. Pansy
17. Judged (Hebrew)	Q. Roxanne
18. From the meadow on the ledge (Old English)	R. Shelley
19. Beautiful one (Irish Gaelic)	S. Tallulah
20. Flattering, industrious (Slavic)	T. Winona

Part II

1. From the black or dark water (Scotch Gaelic)	A. Ammon
2. Famous son (Old Norse)	B. Brice
3. From the high peak (Pictish-Scotch)	C. Carson
4. Royally peaceful, famous (Old Slavic)	D. Douglas
5. Gatekeeper (French)	E. Egan
6. Flaxen-haired (Greek)	F. Flint
7. Treasure-master (Persian)	G. Gaspar
8. Dweller at the fifth son's estate (Old French)	H. Herbert
9. The hidden (Egyptian)	I. Ingemar
10. Stream (Old English)	J. Jesse
11. Champion's son (English)	K. Kent
12. Ardent, fiery one (Irish Gaelic)	L. Linus
13. Smooth, polished one (Latin)	m. Maddox
14. Wealth (Hebrew)	N. Nelson
15. Savior (Spanish)	O. Ogilvie
16. Army man, warrior (Old German)	P. Porter
17. Son of the dweller at a marsh (Middle English)	Q. Quincy
18. The benefactor's son (Old Anglo-Welsh)	R. Salvador
19. White, bright (Old Welsh)	S. Terence
20. Quick one (Celtic-Welsh)	T. Vladimir

34. OUT OF PLACE

Here is how Wells-Fargo asked its passengers in posted notices, to comport themselves more than 100 years ago in cross-country stages.

Adherence to the following rules will insure a pleasant trip for all.

1. Abstinence from liquor is requested, but if you must drink, share the bottle. To do so otherwise makes you appear selfish and un-neighborly.
2. If ladies are present, gentlemen are urged to forego smoking cigars and pipes as the odor of same is repugnant to the Gentle Sex. Chewing tobacco is permitted, but spit WITH the wind, not against it.
3. Gentlemen must refrain from the use of rough language in the presence of ladies and children.
4. Buffalo robes are provided for your comfort during cold weather. Hogging robes will not be tolerated and the offender will be made to ride with the driver.
5. Don't snore loudly while sleeping or use your fellow passenger's shoulder for a pillow; he (or she) may not understand and friction may result.
6. Firearms may be kept on your person for use in emergencies. Do not fire them for pleasure or shoot at wild animals as the sound riles the horses.
7. In the event of runaway horses, remain calm. Leaping from the coach in panic will leave you injured, at the mercy of the elements, hostile Indians and hungry coyotes.
8. Forbidden topics of discussion are stagecoach robberies and Indian uprisings.
9. Gents guilty of unchivalrous behavior toward lady passengers will be put off the stage. It's a long walk back. A word to the wise is sufficient.

When one reads these rules they really don't seem too out of place for passengers in present-day autos, planes, or buses. This quiz asks you to identify the name or item that is most unlike the others: for example, in a listing of Montana, Kentucky, Albany, and Idaho you should have no problem in picking Albany as the out-of-place word.

1. a. Jonathan   b. Kinnard   c. Bing   d. Porter
2. a. Say's Law   b. Hooke's Law   c. Wagner's Law   d. Engel's Law
3. a. Thomas   b. Aldous   c. Julian   d. Charles
4. a. Colby   b. Gerber   c. Coon   d. Minnesota Blue
5. a. Fultons   b. Perkins   c. Pulkova   d. Yerkes
6. a. Mr. Layard   b. Mr. Carter   c. Mr. Winckler   d. Mr. McMahon   e. Mr. Schliemann
7. a. Nicaea   b. Orleans   c. Constance   d. Trent
8. a. Diamond   b. Pearl   c. Nonpareil   d. Jasper   e. Agate   f. Bourgeois
9. a. Timothy   b. Quack   c. Merion   d. Watson
10. a. Marjoram   b. Curie   c. Costmary   d. Lovage   e. Tarragon   f. Sweet Cicely   g. Sage
11. a. Russell   b. Majors   c. Waddell   d. Dingley
12. a. Modulus   b. Coelostat   c. Bolometer   d. Orrery
13. a. Mr. Micawber   b. Dr. Pangloss   c. Cassandra   d. Pollyanna
14. a. Inkerman   b. Trafalgar   c. Balaklava   d. Sevastopol
15. a. Mohawks   b. Onondagas   c. Tuscaroras   d. Oneidas   e. Senecas   f. Delawares   g. Cayugas
16. a. Clovis   b. Conradin   c. Clotaire   d. Dagobert
17. a. Narraganset   b. Bronze   c. White Holland   d. Rouen
18. a. Cosimo   b. Catherine   c. Marguerite   d. Lorenzo
19. a. Fibula   b. Miasma   c. Patella   d. Tibia
20. a. Chester Nimitz   b. George Bancroft   c. Edward Whymper   d. David Farragut

35. PHILATELIC TERMS

The postage stamp arose from the custom of sending packages and mail from post to post. One messenger carried the mail to a certain post or station, where it was picked up by another messenger who carried it to another station. The word "postage" meant the charge for carrying mail. The sender of the letter or package sealed it with wax and stamped the wax with a seal or ring bearing his signature, giving rise to the term "stamp." At first the mail was carried by private couriers, and the charge was based on the number of sheets in a letter and the distance it had to travel.

In the 1830s an Englishman named Rowland Hill suggested that stamps should be used on mail and that the cost of the mail should be determined by the weight. In 1840 Great Britain started to issue postage stamps. It was the first country to do so, and the idea spread rapidly. Zurich and Geneva were the next to issue postage stamps. Brazil issued stamps in 1843, and the United States followed in 1847. Some private letter-carrying services in the United States were issuing stamps in 1843 before the government took over the mails.

There were many post offices in the United States that were located in difficult-to-reach places. The federal government made contracts with private messengers for the delivery of mail to such offices. The messenger guaranteed to pick up mail and deliver it by the swiftest, safest means possible. His route was known as a star route, because post-office records indicated such routes with three stars, or asterisks, which stood for celerity, certainty, and security. Star-route service is not the same as rural free delivery. This is taken care of by civil-service employees. Star routes became less important as railroads were built throughout the country, but when automobiles began to be widely used, railroads stopped serving many places and the number of star routes increased.

See if you can increase your stamp knowledge by trying to match up the description with the correct word.

Part I

1. Any word, inscription, or device placed on a stamp to alter its use or locality or to serve a special purpose
2. A line of small cuts or holes placed between two rows of stamps to facilitate separation
3. Stamps issued in rolls for use in affixing or vending machines
4. Three or more unsevered stamps forming a vertical or horizontal row
5. An unsevered pair of stamps that differ in value, design, or surcharge
6. An unsevered group of stamps at least two stamps wide and two stamps high
7. Small strips of paper gummed on one side and used by collectors to mount their stamps
8. Stamps printed upside down in relation to each other
9. Regular issues of stamps as distinct from commemoratives
10. Designs submitted in stamp form but not accepted for issuance

WORD LIST

A. Block	D. Essays	G. Perforations
B. Coils	E. Hinges	H. Se-tenant
C. Definitives	F. Overprint	I. Strip
		J. Tete-beche

Part II

1. Short consecutive cuts in the paper between rows of stamps to facilitate separation
2. A design or pattern incorporated into the paper during its manufacture
3. Parallel rows of small pyramids impressed or embossed on the stamp in order to break the fibers of the paper so that the cancellation ink will soak in and make washing for reuse impossible
4. A portion of the original sheet cut for sale at the post office
5. A special hand stamp or printed device on a cover to denote the special circumstances in which it was mailed
6. The original steel engraving from which the plates for printing stamps are made
7. An overprint that alters or restates the face value or denomination of the stamp to which it is applied
8. Stamps issued for use in restricted areas by either governments or private carriers
9. Stamps that honor anniversaries, important people, or special events
10. Stamps issued prior to the regular issues or to meet a temporary shortage of regular stamps

WORD LIST

A. Cachet	D. Grill	G. Provisionals
B. Commemoratives	E. Locals	H. Rouletting
C. Die	F. Pane	I. Surcharge
		J. Watermark

36. PHILOSOPHY SCHOOLS AND THEORIES

The Athenian philosopher Socrates was born in 469 B.C. His father Sophroniscus was a statuary; his mother Phaenarete was a midwife. In his youth Socrates followed the profession of his father. His physical constitution was healthy and robust. He was capable of bearing fatigue or hardship and was indifferent to heat or cold. He went barefoot in all seasons of the year, even during the winter campaign at Potidaea, and the same homely clothing sufficed for him in winter as well as in summer. He had a flat nose, thick lips, and prominent eyes. He seems never to have filled any political office until 406 B.C., in which year he was a member of the senate of Five Hundred. At what time Socrates gave up his profession as a statuary we do not know, but it is certain that at least the middle and later part of his life was devoted to teaching. He never opened a school, nor did he, like the Sophists of his time, deliver public lectures. Everywhere — in the marketplace, in the gymnasia, and in the workshops — he sought and found opportunities to awaken and guide boys and men in developing moral consciousness and knowledge. He died with composure and cheerfulness in his 70th year, 399 B.C., after drinking the fatal hemlock.

The logical thing to do in this chapter is to match the definition to the correct work in the list.

1. The belief that God is identical with the universe
2. The belief that the world is capable of improvement and that man has the power to help improve it, a position between optimism and pessimism
3. The doctrine that universal ideas are neither created by finite (human) minds nor entirely separate from absolute mind (God)
4. The doctrine that pleasure is the highest good
5. The principle of living and acting in the interest of others rather than oneself
6. The theory that reality is only appearance
7. The theory that reason alone without the aid of experience can arrive at the basic reality of the universe
8. The belief in only one ultimate reality, whatever its nature
9. The theory that the path to knowledge lies midway between dogmatism and skepticism
10. The belief that the world consists of two radically independent and absolute elements: e.g., good and evil, spirit and matter
11. The denial of objective universal values: man must create values for himself through action, and the self is the ultimate reality
12. The doctrine that man can have no knowledge except of phenomena and that the knowledge of phenomena is relative, not absolute
13. The doctrine that general terms have no corresponding reality either in or out of the mind and are in effect nothing more than words
14. A method that makes practical consequences the test of truth
15. The assertion of a belief without authoritative support

WORD LIST

A. Altruism
B. Conceptualism
C. Criticism
D. Dogmatism
E. Dualism
F. Existentialism
G. Hedonism
H. Meliorism
I. Monism
J. Nominalism
K. Pantheism
L. Phenomenalism
M. Positivism
N. Pragmatism
O. Rationalism

37. QUOTATIONS IN HISTORY

In the preface to the first edition of *Familiar Quotations,* John Bartlett wrote:

"The object of this work is to show, to some extent, the obligations our language owes to various authors for numerous phrases and familiar quotations which have become household words."

This collection, originally made without any view of publication, has been considerably enlarged by additions from an English work on a similar plan, and is now sent forth with the hope that it may be found a convenient book of reference.

Though perhaps imperfect in some respects, it is believed to possess the merit of accuracy, as the quotations have been taken from the original sources. Should this be favorably received, endeavors will be made to make it more worthy of the approbation of the public in a future edition.

Cambridge, May, 1855

The first edition was a thin volume of 258 pages. John Bartlett edited the first nine editions of the book. The ninth edition, published in 1891, had grown to a volume of 1,158 pages, 862 of text and 296 of index. Although Bartlett commented that the ninth edition was the close of the volume's tentative life, another edition appeared in 1914, and yet others in 1937 and 1948. The thirteenth centennial edition appeared in 1955.

Even if you aren't familiar with Bartlett, you should be able to answer some of these 16 questions about quotations in history.

1. To whom is attributed the saying, "I disapprove of what you say but will defend to the death your right to say it"?
2. What 19th-century English historian wrote, "Absolute power corrupts absolutely"?
3. A famous 16th-century French satirist's last will read: "I owe much; I have nothing; the rest I leave to the poor." Who was he?
4. To which English monarch does the following phrase refer: "A prince, whose character is thus marked by every act which may define a tyrant, is unfit to be the ruler of a free people"?
5. Name the 17th-century Englishman who wrote: "Time, place, and action may with pains be wrought, But genius must be born, and never can be taught."
6. Who said, "The tree of liberty must be refreshed from time to time with the blood of patriots and tyrants"?
7. Who said, "I think, therefore I am"?
8. What ancient Greek king is reputed to have said of a certain military victory, "Yes, but if we have another such victory, we are undone"?
9. Name the great 17th-century English scientist who once said of his life, "I do not know what I may appear to the world; but to myself I seem to have been only like a boy playing on the seashore, and diverting myself in now and then finding a smoother pebble or a prettier shell than ordinary, whilst the great ocean of truth lay all undiscovered before me."
10. Who is the author of these lines? "What is happening to our young people: They disrespect their elders, they disobey their parents. They ignore the laws. They riot in the street inflamed with wild notions. Their morals are decaying. What is to become of them?"
11. Identify the speaker in the following farewell: "But it is now time to depart — for me to die, for you to live. But which of us is going to a better state is unknown to everyone but God."
12. Name the writer who in 1835 wrote these words about America and Russia: "Their starting point is different, and their courses are not the same; yet each of them seems marked out by the will of Heaven to sway the destinies of half the globe."
13. Name the English political philosopher who wrote in a 1859 essay: "We can never be sure that the opinion we are endeavoring to stifle is a false opinion; and if we were sure, stifling it would be an evil still."
14. What Roman naturalist wrote, "The only certainty is that nothing is certain"?
15. During what July 1861 battle did General Stonewall Jackson supposedly command, "When you charge, yell like furies"?
16. What English playwright wrote: "Mad dogs and Englishmen go out in the mid-day sun"?

38. RELIGIOUS GROUPS AND PEOPLE

Upon the death of Joseph Smith Brigham Young became the head of the Mormon Church. When the Mormons were driven from their homes at Nauvoo, Illinois, he directed the task of moving 15,000 exiles across Iowa to a new home near Omaha, Nebraska. This haven of refuge was known as Winter Quarters. He led mass migrations to the valley of the Great Salt Lake. Four days after he arrived, Young walked out upon the valley floor, pointed to the ground, and declared, "Here we will build a temple to our God." There the famous Mormon Temple stands today. The city of Salt Lake was laid off in ten-acre blocks with the temple as its center. The streets were 132' wide, the sidewalks 20' wide. Public drinking fountains were three to the block. Trees would be planted by the thousands, while homes with shrubs and gardens would be built on spacious lots.

Many parks, a city hall, and places for public gatherings were to be constructed. A dome-shaped tabernacle, large enough to seat 10,000 people and equipped with the largest organ in the world, was planned. A university, theater, public schools, and places of worship were also in the master plan.

To plant crops, the pioneers used irrigation by damming up the streams flowing from the mountains. By the end of the Civil War Salt Lake Valley had 277 canals irrigating 150,000 acres of tillable farmland.

You already know the answer to question 4 in this chapter. With only 24 questions left, match the name of the religious group or movement with the founder or person closely associated with it.

1. Disciples of Christ
2. Friends (or Quakers)
3. Methodists
4. Mormons (or Latter Day Saints)
5. Christian Scientists
6. Jehovah's Witnesses
7. Adventists
8. Unity
9. Spiritualists
10. Theosophy
11. Church of the New Jerusalem
12. Vedanta Society
13. Salvation Army
14. House of David
15. International Church of the Four Square Gospel
16. I Am
17. Fountain of the World
18. Peace Mission Movement
19. The Oxford Group (or Moral Re-Armament)
20. Psychiana
21. Shakers
22. Pillar of Fire
23. Volunteers of America
24. Anthroposophy
25. The Church Triumphant (or Koreshanity)

A. Emanuel Swedenborg
B. Mary Baker Eddy
C. Father M.J. Divine
D. Aimee Semple McPherson
E. Swami Vivekananda
F. George Fox
G. Frank B. Robinson
H. Ballington and Maude Booth
I. Charles and Myrtle Fillmore
J. William Miller
K. Joseph Smith
L. Krishna Venta
M. Alma White
N. Cyrus R. Teed
O. William Booth
P. Benjamin Franklin Purnell
Q. Charles Taze Russell
R. John Wesley
S. Rudolf Steiner
T. Guy and Edna Ballard
U. Ann Lee
V. Frank Buchman
W. Madame Helena P. Blavatsky
X. Thomas Campbell
Y. Margaret and Kate Fox

39.   SHAKESPEARE AND HISTORY

English records show that on April 26, 1564 a child named William Shakespeare was baptized in the church of Stratford-on-Avon. He married in 1582, left Stratford in 1584, went to London, and became an actor. He began to write plays for his theatrical company. They were well received, and the author made enough money to buy several houses. He was 52 when he died, a well-known but not famous man, perhaps because his writings were only in manuscript.

Because of the range of his knowledge people began to wonder how a simple country actor could have learned so much about life. Some suspected that the brilliant, worldly Earl of Oxford may have written the plays and poems and, not wishing his name to be attached to the then vulgar world of theater, hired the actor William Shakespeare to appear to be the author.

The earliest and probably the best-known substitute proposed was Sir Francis Bacon, lawyer, essayist, and philosopher. An English rector, the Reverend James Wilmot, suggested in 1805 that Sir Francis was the true author of the plays. A large number of other writers have enlarged on this theme in the last century and a half. Many have professed to find startling parallels between the published writings of Shakespeare and Bacon. Most experts discount this and similar theories.

No matter who you think wrote the plays, it shouldn't make any difference to your answers to the next 12 questions.

1. Name the English general who said that he knew English history only as he had learned it from the Histories of Shakespeare.
2. Who was Richard Burbage?
3. What was Sack?
4. What is the only book of the Bible mentioned in Shakespeare?
5. From whom did Shakespeare borrow the stories of Venus and Adonis and the Rape of Lucrece?
6. Who is the real hero of *Julius Caesar?*
7. Name four other English writers who have told the *Troilus and Cressida* story.
8. Hamlet has been compared and contrasted with Orestes in Greek tragedy. With which character in Greek tragedy would you compare Ophelia?
9. What event is said to have prompted the hasty writing of *Macbeth?*
10. Who presided over the baptism of Elizabeth, the future queen, in *Henry VIII?*
11. There are at least four incidents in *Richard II* in which Shakespeare altered the narrative of Holinshed's *Chronicle.* Describe one of them.
12. It has been said that there are four outstanding themes around which Shakespeare's thoughts revolved in the Histories. Name at least two of them.

40. SHAKESPEARE AND NATURE

Some of the loveliest of all legends are attached to the spice rosemary. This herb is for remembrance because, as folklore has it, once upon a time it bore a white flower, which turned to the blue of the Virgin Mary's gown when she hung her linen on the bush to dry during her flight into Egypt. Shakespeare was cognizant of this, for in Act IV, Scene V of *Hamlet* Ophelia says: "There's rosemary, that's for remembrance."

Rosemary was also thought to strengthen the memory and was therefore an emblem of fidelity. This factor is said to have inaugurated the custom of wearing it at weddings. Rosemary, the leaf of an evergreen shrub and similar in appearance to a curved pine needle, has gathered legend after legend. One says that it will grow only in the gardens of the righteous; another, that it will not grow over 6' in height because it grew only to the height of Our Lord and after His death grew only in breadth.

In this quiz you should be able to remember the answer to question 15.

1. Who owned these horses: Roan Barbary, white Surrey, Dobbin?
2. "I had rather be a dog and bay the moon than such a Roman." Who said this about whom?
3. "You may as well say that's a valiant flea that dare eat his breakfast on the lip of a lion." Who said this?
4. "The world is grown so bad/That wrens make prey where eagles dare not perch." Who said this?
5. Who owned these dogs: Ringwood, Lady, Crab?
6. "I am as melancholy as a gib cat or a lugg'd bear." Who said this?
7. "Thus hath the candle sing'd the moth." Who said this?
8. "The smallest worm will turn, being trodden on; And doves will peck in safeguard of their brood." Who said this?
9. "In a cowslip's bell I lie." Who said this?
10. What were pomewaters, bitter sweetings, and leather-coats to Shakespeare?
11. Shakespeare refers to 113 plants. How many of the following common flowers are mentioned by him: foxglove, snapdragon, hollyhock, sweet william, love-lies-bleeding?
12. "Our bodies are our gardens, to the which our wills are gardeners." Who said this?
13. "An oak but with one green leaf on it would have answered her." Who said this of whom?
14. "A bank where the wild thyme blows, Where oxlips and the nodding violet grows." Who knew about this place?
15. Name the two fragrant herbs that Perdita said kept "seeming and savour all the winter long."

41. STATE MOTTOS

State mottos are most often associated with freedom, liberty, justice, union, and growth. These things would be impossible without an agreement as to the actual boundaries of each state. The history of establishing the boundaries of the states ranges from simple agreement to violent bloodshed.

The following specifications were prepared for the monuments on the New York-Connecticut boundary, survey of 1909-1910, and are quoted as examples of adequate marks:

The monuments are to be of good-quality light-colored granite, free from seams or other defects, straight and of full size throughout, not less than 9 nor more than 10 feet in length, 12 inches square 4 feet down from the top, tapering from 12 inches square to not over 15 inches square in the next 1½ feet and not less than 12 inches nor more than 20 inches on any face the rest of the distance. The top and the four sides of each monument for a distance of 4 feet from the top are to be cut smooth at right angles with each other and finished with 6-cut work. The tapering portion to be pointed to a smooth even surface to conform to the dimensions given. The remaining portions to be left as split, but full size, not less than 12 inches square throughout, the bottom to be not less than 12 inches square and substantially at right angles to the sides, and every point of the lower 5 feet of the stone must lie outside the planes of the smooth-cut portion. On one side will be cut the letters "N.Y."; on the opposite side will be cut the letters "CONN." On the third side will be cut the figures "1909." Additional similar letters shall be cut as may be ordered. The letters "N.Y." and "CONN." are to be 5 inches high; the figures to be 4 inches high. All letters to be cut with V-shaped indentations at least 1/3 inch deep.

These monuments were set in concrete bases 4' square and 5' deep. The only mark that you have to make in this quiz is to identify the state with its motto.

Part I

1. Alabama
2. Delaware
3. Indiana
4. Louisiana
5. New Hampshire
6. North Dakota
7. Rhode Island
8. Utah

A. Live free or die
B. The crossroads of America
C. Industry
D. We dare defend our rights (Audemus jura nostra defenders)
E. Liberty and union, now and forever; one and inseparable
F. Union, justice, and confidence
G. Liberty and independence
H. Hope

Part II

1. Arizona
2. Florida
3. Iowa
4. Mississippi
5. New Jersey
6. Ohio
7. South Dakota
8. Vermont

A. In God we trust
B. Under God the people rule
C. Our liberties we prize and our rights we will maintain
D. With God, all things are possible
E. Freedom and unity
F. God enriches (Ditat Deus)
G. By valor and arms (Virtute et armis)
H. Liberty and prosperity

Part III

1. Arkansas
2. Georgia
3. Kansas
4. Nebraska
5. New Mexico
6. Oregon
7. Tennessee
8. Virginia

A. To the stars through difficulties (Ad astra per aspera)
B. Thus always to tyrants (Sic semper tyrannis)
C. The people rule (Regnat populus)
D. The Union
E. Wisdom, justice, and moderation
F. Agriculture, commerce
G. It grows as it goes (Crescit eundo)
H. Equality before the law

Part IV

1. California
2. Illinois
3. Kentucky
4. Nevada
5. North Carolina
6. Pennsylvania
7. Texas
8. Wisconsin

A. Virtue, liberty, and independence
B. United we stand, divided we fall
C. Forward
D. Friendship
E. All for our country
F. State sovereignty, national union
G. To be, rather than to seem (Esse quam videri)
H. I have found it (Eureka)

42. TEXTILES AND FABRICS

The following office rules were drawn up by an English cotton mill in 1852.

1. Godliness, cleanliness and punctuality are the necessities of good business.
2. This firm has reduced the hours of work, and the clerical staff will now have to be present only between the hours of 7 A.M. and 6 P.M. on weekdays.
3. Daily prayers will be held each morning in the main office. The clerical staff will be present.
4. Clothing must be of a sober nature. The clerical staff will not disport themselves in raiment of bright colors, nor will they wear hose unless in good repair.
5. A stove is provided for the benefit of the clerical staff. Coal and wood must be kept in the locker. It is recommended that each member of the clerical staff bring in 4 pounds of coal each day during cold weather.
6. No member of the clerical staff may leave the room without permission from Mr. Rogers. The calls of nature are permitted and the clerical staff may use the garden below the second gate. The area must be kept in good order.
7. No talking is allowed during business hours.
8. The craving for tobacco, wines or spirits is a human weakness and as such is forbidden to all members of the clerical staff.
9. Now that the hours of business have been so drastically reduced, the partaking of food is allowed only between 11:30 A.M. and noon, but work will not, on any account, cease.
10. The new increased weekly wages are as hereunder detailed. Junior boys (up to 11 years) 11 cents; Boys (to 14 years) 25 cents; Juniors 56 cents; Junior clerks, $1.03; Clerks, $1.29; Senior Clerks (after 15 years with owners) $2.52. The owners recognize the generosity of the new Labour Laws, but will expect a great rise in output of work to compensate for these near utopian conditions.

You will have your own utopia if you manage to correctly match all the definitions with the words in both parts of this quiz.

Part I

1. Glazed cotton fabric often printed with gay figures and large flower designs, named from a Hindu word meaning "spotted"
2. A firm, twill-weave cotton fabric first made in Nimes, France
3. A fine, plain-weave fabric that is smooth on both sides, usually with a sheen to its surface
4. A form of the rib-knitting stitch modified for tucking on one or both sets of needles; also a sweater style referring to a three-button coat sweater with either a V- or a round neck
5. A very thin, transparent, stiff, and wiry cotton muslin used for dresses, neckwear, and trimmings
6. A rough-surfaced woolen material with a homespun surface effect, originally made by hand in the homes of country people near the river that separates England from Scotland
7. An all-wool fabric woven of woolen or worsted yarns and with a softly napped surface, from the Welsh word *gwlamen* meaning "allied to wool"
8. Woolen or worsted fabric similar to serge but not as likely to wear shiny due to a slightly rough-napped surface
9. A soft, lightweight wool material in plain weave with a napped, fleecy surface, usually light-colored, used for negligees, infants' wear, and nuns' habits
10. Soft, plain-weave cotton fabric of low thread count, similar to tobacco cloth and also known as gauze
11. Coarse, canvas-like fabric made of jute, hemp, or cotton; also called gunny
12. A yarn-dyed plain-weave cotton fabric woven in stripes, plaids, and checks
13. A fine, soft cotton cloth woven of softly twisted yarns, similar to nainsook but slightly heavier and with a duller surface
14. A twill-weave fabric made of wool or silk yarns with a characteristic prominent diagonal wale on both sides of the cloth
15. Highly sized stiff fabric used as a foundation to support the edge of a hem or puffed sleeve

WORD LIST

A. Albatross
B. Burlap
C. Cardigan
D. Cheesecloth
E. Cheviot
F. Chintz
G. Crinoline
H. Denim

I. Flannel
J. Gingham
K. Longcloth
L. Organdy
M. Serge
N. Taffeta
O. Tweed

Part II

1. A hard fiber larger and stiffer than flax, hemp, or jute, grown on large plantations in Java, Haiti, Kenya, and Central America
2. Hair from the Angora goat
3. A yarn with a fuzzy pile protruding from all sides in a woven fabric, used for filling in cloth, embroidery fringes, and tassels
4. A tightly woven steep-twilled material, Spanish in origin, named from the Spanish word meaning "protection against the elements," distinguished by a marked raised diagonal weave on the right side
5. Firm, glossy, patterned fabric with a jacquard weave, first brought to the western world by Marco Polo in the 13th century
6. Cotton fabric covered with loops on one or both sides, made by using two sets of warp threads and one set of filling threads, extremely water-absorbent
7. An old term for a plain-woven, printed cotton cloth similar to percale and often sold as such
8. Soft, plain-weave sheer fabric, either silk or rayon, with either a soft or a stiff finish
9. Fabrics made of the extremely soft wool of Indian goats
10. A twill-weave fabric similar to gabardine but with a more pronounced diagonal rib on the right side
11. Strong, lustrous yarn or fabric of smooth-surfaced flax fibers, either in plain weave or a damask weave
12. Tightly woven cotton or linen fabric similar to canvas with plain and rib weaves
13. Durable fabric in a plain weave with fine cross-ribs (made by using warp threads that are finer than the weft, or filling, threads), similar to broadcloth but with a heavier rib, made of silk, cotton, synthetics, wool, or a combination of these fibers
14. Rich, jacquard-woven fabric with an all-over interwoven design of raised figures or flowers
15. Durable cotton or rayon cut-pile fabric woven with either a wide or narrow wale (formed with an extra filling); the foundation of the fabric can be either plain or twill weave

WORD LIST

A. Brocade
B. Calico
C. Cashmere
D. Chenille
E. Chiffon
F. Corduroy
G. Damask
H. Duck
I. Gabardine
J. Linen
K. Mohair
L. Poplin
M. Sisal
N. Terry
O. Whipcord

43. TRANSPORTATION

Russia's Trans-Siberian Railway has the world's longest continuous train journey, from Moscow to Nakhodka on the Sea of Japan. Starting from Moscow the trip to Korov is 591 miles through endless green fields and coniferous forests. For hundreds of miles more the line goes to Sverdlovsk, part of a huge industrial complex on the east side of the Urals. A leg of 1,420 miles includes Krasnoyarsk on the River Yenesei. After crossing the Siberian plain — Omsk and Novosibirsk — where there is an immense hydroelectric complex, the Yenesei turns into a sea 250 miles long. From here a trip of 676 miles through mountains leads to Irkutsk. Here is the biggest hydroelectric complex in the world, with an artificial sea 350 miles long. The line then skirts Lake Baikal, the clearest and deepest — 5,314' — in the world. After this comes a 183-mile trip to Ulan Ude and to Chita — another 347 miles — on the Ingoda River in Transbaikal, a beautiful region with Rocky Mountain-type mountains. After skirting the Chinese border for hundreds of miles the train rolls into Khabarovsk (another 1,445 miles on), a city of 500,-000 people on the Amur River. From here it goes on to Nakhodka, where Russian steamers leave for Yokohama, Osaka, and Hong Kong.

It is hoped that you don't take nearly as long to answer the next 20 questions about transportation.

1. What was the name of the airplane in which Wiley Post soloed around the world?
2. Under what river is the Holland Tunnel?
3. What was the Blenheim?
4. What dirigible made the first commercial transatlantic flight?
5. Who flew from Italy to the Chicago World's Fair with a fleet of 24 seaplanes?
6. What did Juan de la Cierva invent?
7. Who made the first solo flight around the world?
8. What was the original rate when airmail was established on May 15, 1918?
9. Did the Graf Zeppelin ever circle the globe?
10. Did the Model A supersede the Model T in 1918, 1927, 1929, or 1934?
11. Who produced the Airflow?
12. What did Socony stand for?
13. Who produced the 1936 Terraplane?
14. What railroad advertised that it "carried more passengers and handled more freight than any other railroad in America"?
15. What was the 1923 MacFarland noted for?
16. What was the U.S.S. Langley's claim to fame?
17. What was the transmission system used in Ford autos in the twenties?
18. To whom was Pilot License #1 issued?
19. Who mistakenly piloted the Flying Crate to Ireland?
20. What was the name of the airplane in which Richard E. Byrd crossed the Atlantic?

44. UNDERWORLD SLANG

The word "hobo" is believed to be a contraction of "hoe boy." Any one or more of six major causes can produce a hobo: seasonal work and unemployment; inability to hold a steady job because of low mentality, restlessness, physical handicaps, alcoholism, drug addiction, or advancing years; personality defects that make steady work impossible; personal crises; discrimination because of race, creed, or color; and wanderlust. Of two equal jobs the hobo will usually head for the one farthest away. He constantly seeks variety and experience — something to brag about. That is one of the basic appeals of the hobo camp, or jungle. The jungle is the service center where he can eat the community mulligan stew, wash his clothes, sleep, and exchange travel information on easy towns and hard cops.

Time was when the knights of the road even had a secret grip, a sign of recognition and a danger signal. The handshake consisted of pressing your thumbnail in the back of the other hobo's hand. You knew that you had met a fellow hobo if he responded by taking your middle finger and forefinger in his grip. If you didn't get that close, you could still identify a kindred roamer. All you had to do was let him see you scratch your chin with your right hand, then hold the lobe of your right ear between the index finger and thumb of the same hand. If he placed his clenched fist over his heart, he recognized you. And if a cop or an enemy were approaching, you could signal a warning by pressing the back of your head with either hand and then putting the back of the same hand to your mouth.

Today communication concentrates mainly on secret code signs of the open road. Scrawled on sidewalk, fence, telegraph pole, water tank, storefront, house, or barn, they speak a language all their own. Some of the signs relating to houses are: a T, which means that they'll feed you if you work; a circle, nothing doing; a cat, a kind woman; a cross, sanctimonious; two vertical lines, the sky is the limit; an inverted triangle, spoiled by too many tramps; and a triangle with arms out to the sides, you may be shot.

To do your honest day's work in this quiz, match the 26 slang terms with their meanings.

Slang Term	Meaning
1. Belcher	A. Stolen-goods handler
2. Betty	B. Parole
3. Bleeder	C. Swindler
4. Booster	D. Arrest
5. Buster	E. Woman
6. Candy	F. Decoy
7. Chatterbox	G. Shoplifter
8. Cush	H. Informer
9. Dip	I. Wallets
10. Fence	J. Warning
11. Flag	K. Police chase
12. Fry	L. Counterfeit money
13. Gat	M. Lawyer
14. Grifter	N. Convict
15. Heat	O. Skeleton key
16. Moll	P. Blackjack
17. Mouthpiece	Q. Firearm
18. Nippers	R. Jewelry
19. Peter	S. Handcuffs
20. Pinch	T. Freight train
21. Queer	U. Machine gun
22. Raincheck	V. Electrocute
23. Rattler	W. Safe
24. Shill	X. Money
25. Sleepers	Y. Extortionist
26. Stiff	Z. Pickpocket

45. WHAT DO THEY HAVE IN COMMON?

Jefferson Davis touched off a United States camel caper when, as secretary of war, he was faced with serious transportation problems during the 1840s because of rapid territorial expansion. Davis proposed that the army use camels to transport men, mail, and material; help fight Indians; and hasten the settlement of the new land. He argued that the Southwest was similar in geography to the Near East, where camels had been the major form of transportation since biblical times. With the idea that camels could be introduced, Congress appropriated $30,000 in 1855 to get the great camel experiment under way. Two young officers, Army Major Henry C. Wayne and Navy Lieutenant David D. Porter, were dispatched to Egypt and Asia on a camel-buying mission. The officers soon learned about the ins-and-outs of camel trading. They finally loaded their ship with 33 one-humped camels, purchased for approximately $250 each. Birth increased the lot to 34 by the time the ship landed at Indianaola, Texas on May 14, 1856. A year later 41 more camels arrived. The animals were kept near San Antonio, Texas and at first were used to carry supplies and equipment between army posts. From there they were removed to Camp Verde, about 60 miles southwest of San Antonio, where a permanent camel post was located.

It was found that the camels could easily carry 600 pounds each, cover 30 to 40 miles a day, climb mountain trails, feed on plants and prickly cacti that no other animal would eat, and go without water for six to ten days. Camel caravans were sent to Fort Tejon, California and made several pack trips between there and Albuquerque, New Mexico.

The camels' army caretakers disliked them, however, as did the transportation mainstays of the Southwest, horses and mules. Furthermore, camels were useless in fighting Indians because of their unimpressive 2-miles per hour gait.

At the outbreak of the Civil War the great experiment was discontinued. Some of the camels were sold at auction and ended up in zoos and circuses. Part of the herd, however, wandered off into the Arizona desert.

This chapter is also concerned with things in common. Identify the character, event, or thing.

1. What did these men have in common: The Old Man in the Corner, Philip Trent, Lord Peter Wimsey, Max Carrados, and John Thorndyke, K.C.?
2. What did these people have in common: Captain Molyneux, Dorian, Adrian, and Chanel?
3. What did these men have in common: John Howard Lawson, Frederick Lonsdale, Sidney Howard, and Jacinto Benavente?
4. What did these men have in common: Alf Shrubb, Tom Longboat, Hannes Kolehmainen, and Jean Bouin?
5. What have these actors had in common: Sheldon Lewis, John Barrymore, Conrad Veidt, Fredric March, and Spencer Tracy?
6. What did these have in common: Pantage, Orpheum, Poli, Loew, and Proctor?
7. What did these people have in common: Myra Hess, Jose Iturbi, Josef Hoffman, and Vladimir de Pachmann?
8. What do these actors have in common: George Kuwa, Kamiyama Sojin, E. L. Park, Warner Oland, Sidney Toler, and Roland Winters?
9. What did these have in common: Liberty, Packard, Curtiss, Wright, and Lawrence?
10. What do these have in common: Raymond & Whitcomb, Frank Co., Clark Co., and Gates Co.?
11. What did these men have in common: Edward Hope, Keith Preston, Jake Falstaff, Ted Robinson, J. E. House, and Heywood Broun?
12. What did these men have in common: Bert Savoy, Dave Montgomery, Joe Weber, and Bobbie Clark?
13. What did these men have in common: J. Howard McGrath, Tom C. Clark, Francis Biddle, Robert H. Jackson, and Frank Murphy?
14. What do these people have in common: Burleigh Grimes, Charley Root, Eddie Rommel, Howard Ehmke, and Urban Faber?
15. What have these actors had in common: Emil Jannings, Adolphe Menjou, Walter Huston, Ray Milland, Ray Walston, Laird Cregar, and Claude Rains?

46. WHAT IN THE WORLD?

The first hot dogs are said to have been made by a butcher in Frankfurt, Germany in 1852. Tradition says that he shaped them like his dog, a dachshund. At about the same time a Viennese developed a similar sausage that was named wienerwurst, or Vienna sausage. In the United States the first franks were sold at Coney Island in 1871 by Charles Feltmann, a butcher from Frankfurt. Feltmann's name is almost forgotten, but one of his employees, Nathan Handwerker, established a Coney Island hot-dog stand that is still a famous hangout.

Although Feltmann introduced hot dogs in the United States and Handwerker helped popularize them, two expositions in 1893 and 1904, respectively, in different cities — Chicago and St. Louis — calimed to have spread their fame nationally.

But it took a cartoonist, Tad Dorgan, to change the name to hot dog. He supposedly invented the nickname because he couldn't spell dachshund, the word used by vendors at football games at the New York Polo Grounds in 1900.

Small meat companies still tailor hot dogs to regional preferences, while bigger manufacturers, whose products are distributed nationally, have standardized their formulas.

Unlike the hot dog, frankfurter, or wiener, many geographical terms have different meanings. The statements below refer to three possible meanings of one geographical word. Of these, one or two may be correct.

1. Etna, a volcano in Sicily is
   a. A case for cigarettes   b. Fluid rock   c. A vessel for heating liquids
2. Madras, a city in India, is
   a. A large, bright kerchief   b. A sweet wine   c. A rattan cane
3. Geneva, a city in Switzerland, is
   a. A black academic gown   b. An Alpine variety of gentian   c. A kind of gin
4. Inverness, a county in Scotland, is
   a. A two-seated pleasure carriage   b. A full, sleeveless cape   c. A raincoat
5. Ankara, capital of Turkey, is
   a. An aromatic bitter   b. An inflammatory infection   c. A woolen cloth or shawl
6. Hamburg, a German seaport, is
   a. A breed of small domestic fowl   b. A seasoned pork chop   c. A variety of cattle
7. Toledo, a city in Spain, is
   a. A fine-tempered sword   b. A pink rose   c. A reversible linen fabric
8. Astrakhan, a city in Russia, is
   a. A carpet of long pile   b. A long-haired dog   c. A long, curled fur
9. Arras, a city in France, is
   a. A kind of police dog   b. A wall tapestry   c. An ardent spirit
10. Winchester, a cathedral city in England, is
    a. A sharp, pungent sauce   b. A sporting firearm   c. A traveling bag
11. Wellington, capital of New Zealand, is
    a. A brand of cattle   b. A high boot   c. A hunting hound
12. Holland, a European kingdom, is
    a. A brand of wine   b. A kind of fowl   c. Unbleached linen
13. Boston, capital of Massachusetts, is
    a. A heavy shoe   b. A card game for four   c. A form of waltz
14. Panama, a Central American nation, is
    a. A fine straw hat   b. A very long cigarette   c. A sweetened bread dish
15. Amazon, the largest South American river, is
    a. An annoying ant   b. A bee queen   c. A tall, strong woman
16. Berlin, capital of East Germany, is
    a. Fine-grained wood   b. A four-wheeled carriage   c. A canoe
17. Troy, a ruined city in Asia Minor, is
    a. A city in New York   b. A system of weight   c. A very heavy cigar
18. Jersey, a Channel Island, is
    a. A fine woolen yarn   b. A wagon   c. A breed of cattle

47. WHAT'S IN A NAME?

According to history cottage cheese was "invented" on a camel's back. After a long day in the saddle, a Middle Eastern trader opened his goatskin bag for a drink of milk. Instead of milk he found solid white curds. The curds are known today by such names as cottage cheese, pot cheese, farmer cheese, and Dutch cheese. Desert-sun cooking and camel-back stirring have been replaced by scientific cheese-making techniques. Goatskin bags have given way to sanitary, decorative, reusable containers.

Cottage-cheese making is a daily project in many dairy plants. Its good flavor, availability, and convenience have made it almost as much a staple as bread and butter. When you shop for cottage cheese, you find it labeled "creamed," "partially creamed," and "dry"; it may be "small curd" or "large curd" and it may have vegetables or fruits added. Both creamed and dry cottage cheese are made from the drained, washed, and salted curd of skim milk. Creamed cottage cheese has sweet pasteurized cream added. No cream is added to dry cottage cheese. Any cottage cheese may be small- or large-curd. Small-curd is sometimes called "country-style" or "old-fashioned." The curds are firm and hold together on a plate. Large-curd cottage cheese is softer.

In most of the next 20 questions you won't have so many possible names for one subject to contend with. Keep saying cheese.

1. The 9th, 25th, and 27th presidents of the United States had the same first name. What was it?
2. a. How many kings of England were named Richard?
   b. How many French kings were named Francis?
   c. How many Scottish kings were named James?
3. The French have traditionally been ruled by three royal lines, one of which was the Carolingian. Name the other two.
4. Two members of Franklin D. Roosevelt's cabinet held their offices throughout the entire period of his presidency. Name them.
5. Name the last premier of France before Petain.
6. Name the famous Athenian statesman, the Athenian dramatist, and the Stagirian philosopher whose names all begin with the letters "A-R-I-S-T."
7. Four members of the Curie family won Nobel Prizes in chemistry and physics. Give their first names.
8. In the American colonial period four wars involving the colonists bore the names of kings or queens. Name the wars.

9. If the French Sun King met the French Spider King, who would meet whom?

10. A desperado named Jack McCall shot and killed a famous American in Deadwood, Dakota Territory. Whom did he shoot?

11. Name the beloved of each of the following:
    a. Orpheus
    b. Pygmalion
    c. Psyche
    d. Baucis
    e. Pyramus

12. King Pelias was warned to beware of a man wearing one sandal. Who was that man?

13. This Norwegian accepted an important political office in 1940 and consequently gave the English language a new word. What's his name?

14. The names Dingley, McKinley, and Underwood are attached to a certain type of legislation. What is it?

15. Identify the two men after whom the seventh and eighth months of our calendar were named.

16. Four surnames have been shared by more than one president of the United States. What are they?

17. One of two major 15th-century French factions had the same name as a well-known brandy, the other that of a full-bodied red wine. Name these factions.

18. Name the country in which each of these parties or groups played an important part:
    a. The Girondists
    b. The Chartists
    c. The Carlists
    d. The Covenanters
    e. The Grangers

19. Name the conflict with which each of the following historians has become closely associated:
    a. Thomas Carlyle
    b. Bruce Catton
    c. Herodotus
    d. Sir George Otto Trevelyan

20. By what initials do we know the French agents Hottinguer, Hauteval, and Bellamy?

48. WINES, SPIRITS, AND DRINKS

No one can say for sure where the story of spirits begins. Every civilization had its liquor. An Egyptian carving depicts distilling apparatus, and shahs of India sipped liquors made from flowers in 800 B.C. Aristotle mentions liquor, and legend has it that Alexander the Great passed the first loving cup as a peace gesture between Macedonians and Persians. It is said that the Aztecs greeted Cortez with offerings of liquor. George Washington was one of the early American distillers. In both trade and war liquor figured in the early history of the United States. In fact, rum has been called the real spirit of '76.

The cocktail got its name at Dobbs Ferry, New York in 1777. In a burst of patriotism barmaid Betsy Flannagan served Washington's officers a special drink made from rum, rye, and fruit juices, decorated by tail feathers from a Tory neighbor's plump rooster. Inspired, a French soldier in the group declared a toast: "Vive le coq's tail!" Thus a legend began.

The word "whiskey" evolved from *uisge* or *usque,* both of Celtic origin. As early as the 12th century the Irish drank *uisge beatha*; the Scots called it *uisgebah.* Either way the term means "water of life."

In the famous Whiskey Rebellion in western Pennsylvania distillers went west to Kentucky. One of the first stills was near Georgetown, Bourbon County, and the product was called Bourbon County Whiskey.

A 17th-century professor at Holland's Leyden University, experimenting with distilling, is credited with discovering *genievre,* French for "juniper," the berry that gives gin its flavor. The English shortened the name to gin. Both Russia and Poland claim to be the birthplace of vodka, but its name stems from the Russian, meaning "little water." At one time vodka was made from potatoes, but American vodkas are made from grains.

In the 1880s in St. Louis early railroaders used a ball on a high pole to signal engineers to speed up. This was called a highball. Trainmen, always on a fast schedule, only had time for a quick drink, which usually was whiskey and water. They named it the highball.

You don't have to catch a train for this one. Match the descriptions with the words in each of two parts, the first on spirits and drinks, the second on wine.

Part I

1. Caraway and anise seeds and other herb flavors
2. Orange-flavored, made of dried orange peel, from Dutch West Indies
3. Sweet white dessert wine
4. Wine flavored with numerous herbs, barks, flowers, leaves, and seeds, 15% to 20% alcoholic content
5. Colorless curacao but less sweet
6. A dry, bitter type of Spanish sherry
7. A French anise-flavored liqueur and absinthe substitute
8. A yellow Italian liqueur, 80 proof
9. Dry, tart red table wine, usually sold in straw-colored bottles
10. A type of Spanish sherry, usually dry, sometimes slightly sweet
11. A reddish, sweet liqueur made from the berry of the blackthorn bush
12. California pink-amber dessert wine, less sweet than port
13. An aged, colorless Mexican liquor of high proof made from the mescal plant
14. Nonalcoholic syrup of pomegranates or red currants, used as a flavoring
15. White, pink, or red sparkling wine, dry, medium-sweet, or sweet
16. French aperitif made from aromatics with a slight quinine taste
17. A golden, spicy liqueur with an angelica-oil base, containing dozens of herbs, spices, and seeds, honey, and brandy
18. A golden liqueur with a Scotch malt-whiskey base, flavored with spices and honey

WORD LIST

A. Amontillado	H. Dubonnet	O. Tequila
B. Angelica	I. Galliano	P. Tokay
C. Benedictine	J. Grenadine	Q. Triple sec
D. Champagne	K. Kummel	R. Vermouth
E. Chianti	L. Montilla	
F. Curacao	M. Pernod	
G. Drambuie	N. Sloe gin	

Part II

1. Tasting piquantly of its grape
2. Partial or complete absence of sugar
3. One who loves good foods and drink
4. Having no harshness of taste
5. Desirable quality in red wines from tannin in skins and seeds
6. A California or other wine named for its variety of grape
7. The science of wine making
8. Consistency, thickness, or substance in a wine
9. Appetizer wine flavored with herbs
10. A general type of after dinner wine
11. A continuous blending process combining the finest of several years' vintages of sherry or port
12. Well-matured, soft, ripe
13. Each year's harvest of grapes and the wines therefrom
14. Examining a bottled wine's clarity by holding it in front of a light
15. The blush on grapes containing natural yeasts for fermentation
16. Wine perfumes formed by the slow chemical interaction of the acids and alcohol in wine
17. Having agreeable fruit acidity
18. A yeast-aging process for sherry
19. That part of a wine's fragrance due to aging rather than the grape
10. A segment of the wine branch used to root new vines
21. A wine at maturity, at its best
22. Wine fragrance from the grape used
23. A person well-versed in a subject such as wine
24. Crushed grape pulp and juice for fermenting
25. The pure spirit distilled from the wine of fresh grapes

WORD LIST

A. Aperitif	J. Cutting	R. Mellow
B. Aroma	K. Dry	S. Must
C. Astringency	L. Oenology	T. Ripe
D. Bloom	M. Esters	U. Smooth
E. Body	N. Flor	V. Solera
F. Bouquet	O. Fruity	W. Tart
G. Brandy	P. Generic	X. Varietal
H. Candling	Q. Gourmet	Y. Vintage
I. Connoisseur		

49. WHO SAID IT?

Peter Mark Roget was an English physician who was born in 1779 and died in 1869. He liked to make lists of words as a hobby and to group them together when they were related to one another. Some were related because they were synonyms, such as grand and impressive; some because they were antonyms, such as dry and moist; some because they were reminders of one another, such as brother and sister. Altogether Roget made a thousand different categories of related words. Every word he knew or could find in the dictionaries was classified in one or more of these categories.

Roget's list of words was published in 1852. He called the book a thesaurus, or treasury, of words. Since that time dozens of editors, beginning with Roget's son, have revised the original *Thesaurus,* added to it, and brought it up to date. Every edition is still called *Roget's Thesaurus* in honor of the man who first had the idea.

The idea in this chapter is to identify the familiar statement with the person who is credited with saying it.

1. "I never met a man I didn't like."
2. "The fog comes on little cat feet."
3. "Nobody shoots at Santa Claus."
4. "Who put pineapple juice in my pineapple juice?"
5. "You ain't heard nothing yet, folks."
6. "Beulah, peel me a grape."
7. "I want to be alone."
8. "I should of stood in bed."
9. "Well, I'll be a dirty bird!"
11. "A man may be down but he's never out."
12. "When more and more people are thrown out of work, unemployment results."
13. "Gentlemen always seem to remember blondes."
14. "The Era of Wonderful Nonsense."
15. "Mad dogs and Englishmen go out in the mid-day sun."
16. "A big butter-and-egg man."
17. "Every man is a king."
18. "That's all there is: there isn't any more."

50. THE WILD WEST

The gunfighters lasted for about two decades, through the seventies and eighties, and then faded from the American scene. The Daltons were about the last of these violent men. Wyatt Earp lived into the twenties, but John Ringo, the Clantons, Luke Short, Doc Holliday, Ben Thompson, Wild Bill Hickok, John Wesley Hardin, Bill Longley, Billy the Kid, and the rest of them were pushing up daisies by then. Legends grew up and rooted firmly in American folklore. The strength of these legends can be demonstrated by the fact that William S. Hart of silent-movie fame paid $25,000 for Billy the Kid's pistol.

The gunfighter was a special breed of man, proud and arrogant, sometimes quiet and shy, but above all an egotist. He believed himself to be superior to any man alive, and he went on and on proving it by fomenting fights by swagger and brag and other means or by protecting his glory from gun-happy kids.

A. M. King, Wyatt Earp's old deputy, states that the fast-draw artist of today shoots against his robot machine, a dangerous man. An ungodly nerve was always part of any gunfighter's makeup. This coolness was the thing that licked many a man. King says of Wyatt: "Not too fast with that long Buntline, but with devilish determination and a cool nerve he rarely missed. I've seen him in action and know."

This chapter isn't a shootout, and you don't need nerves of steel. Choose from the multiple-choice answers offered.

1. The last territory to join the Union was
   a. Oklahoma   b. New Mexico   c. Arizona
2. Jesse James lived in St. Joseph, Missouri under the alias
   a. Robert Ford   b. Sam Bass   c. Thomas Howard
3. The first good road to the far West was the
   a. Oregon Trail   b. Santa Fe Trail   c. National Pike
4. Geronimo surrendered in 1884 to
   a. General Crook   b. General Custer   c. Colonel Mackenzie
5. The first sheriff of Cochise County (Tombstone, Arizona) was
   a. Pat Garret   b. Wyatt Earp   c. Johnny Behan
6. In 1873, a Colt .44 revolver sold for
   a. $32.50   b. $50   c. $20
7. Black Bart was a
   a. Peace officer   b. Stage bandit   c. Train robber
8. The West's famous hanging judge was
   a. Isaac Charles Parker   b. Roger Brooke Taney   c. Roy Bean
9. Dodge City's prosperity was based on
   a. Gold and silver   b. Gambling and sin   c. Buffalo and cattle
10. James Butler (Wild Bill) Hickok was shot by
    a. John Wesley Harcin   b. Jack McCall   c. Clay Allison
11. The Lost Dutchman mine is in
    a. Nevada   b. Montana   c. Arizona
12' The most popular hat of the 1880s was the
    a. Stetson   b. Derby   c. Flat-brimmed Mormon
13. Dr. John (Doc) Holliday's profession was
    a. Surgeon   b. Dentist   c. Veterinarian
14. A yellow-back was a
    a. Cheap novel   b. Yellow-fever patient   c. coward
15. Gold was discovered at Sutter's mill, California in
    a. 1879   b. 1848   c. 1849
16. The Pony Express carried on business for
    a. 4 years   b. 19 months   c. 1 year

51. WOMEN IN HISTORY

Two important incidents helped to set Pierre Curie and his wife Marie Curie on a lifetime search. William Conrad Rontgen had discovered rays of unparalleled penetrative power, which, in a talk before the Berlin Physical Society in 1896, he called "x rays." Shortly thereafter Henri Antoine Becquerel accidentally left a piece of uranium ore on a sensitized photographic plate and discovered that it reacted to the ore as if it had been exposed to light. Becquerel suspected an element at work that was more powerful than the uranium in the ore and suggested to Marie Curie that she search for it. During two years of chemically separating the constituents of a ton of pitchblende the Curies isolated an element a hundredfold more active than uranium, which they called polonium. They continued separating constituents until they obtained from the mineral pitchblende a fraction of a gram of a salt of radium. In 1910 Marie Curie obtained metallic radium by electrolyzing a solution of radium chloride with a mercury cathode. The discovery of the radioactive power of radium and similar elements had far-reaching effects in the fields of heat, medicine, atomic science, and many others.

The 20 questions in this quiz pertain to women. See if you can choose the correct answers.

1. Name the first woman to hold a United States cabinet position.
2. Queen Victoria died in (a) 1891 (b) 1901 (c) 1914
3, What popular dessert was named for a famous woman opera singer?
4. Who is the only woman who has been awarded the Nobel Prize twice?
5. What was Priscilla's last name before she married John Alden?
6. Her maiden name was Elizabeth Griscom. What was her more famous married name?
7. Who was the daughter of Powhatan?
8. Bloody Mary reigned in England in what century?
9. Who was the woman who said: "I killed one man to save a hundred thousand; a villain to save innocents; a savage wild-beast, to give repose to my country. I was a Republican before the Revolution; I never wanted energy"?
10. With what war do you associate each of the following women?
    a. Edith Cavell
    b. Molly Pitcher
    c. Florence Nightingale
    d. Helen of Troy
    e. Tokyo Rose
    f. Dolly Madison
11. To which country was Clare Booth Luce appointed United States ambassador in 1953?
12. Which congresswoman ran for the Democratic presidential nomination in 1972?
13. Who is often called the Virgin Queen?
14. What is the name of the fictional heroine of the book for which Kate Douglas Wiggin is remembered?
15. This lady editor wrote articles in the 1850s in favor of a new form of sports attire for ladies; in time, her name became associated with these garments. Who was she?
16. What was Jacqueline Kennedy Onassis's maiden name?
17. This religious liberal was banished from Massachusetts Bay Colony for "traducing the ministers and their ministry" in 1637. Who was she?
18. Name the Greek woman who accompanied Alexander the Great on his Asiatic campaign and is said to have incited Alexander to burn down the Persian palace at Persepolis.
19. This English novelist who never married was born at Steventon Parsonage, Hampshire. Can you name her?
20. Which queen of France was called the Widow Capet?

52. WRAPUP — ODDS-AND-ENDS

Independence Hall, one of the most famous American landmarks, stands on Chestnut Street in Philadelphia. It was built in 1735 and used as the state house for more than 60 years. Philadelphia was the capital of Pennsylvania until 1799. It was also the capital of the country from 1790 until 1800. In this picturesque old state house, now called Independence Hall and carefully restored to its original appearance, the Continental Congress met. Here Washington was made commander-in-chief of the American army in 1775, and here the Declaration of Independence was adopted on July 4, 1776. Until recently it housed the famous Liberty Bell, with its significant and prophetic motto, "Proclaim liberty throughout all the land to all the inhabitants thereof." The bell was brought from England in 1752, and the inscription proclaiming liberty put on a recast of it in 1753. The Revolutionary War did not break out until 1775, and indeed George III did not come to the throne until 1760 — seven years after the famous bell had "proclaimed liberty."

In this last potpourri quiz, ring out your answers carefully.

1. Zabaglione is a
   a. Musical instrument
   b. Japanese garment
   c. Kind of dessert
2. What are young pilchards called?
3. In what sequence did the following conferences take place?
   a. Yalta
   b. Cairo
   c. Casablanca
4. The United States adopted Daylight Savings Time in
   a. 1910
   b. 1918
   c. 1939
5. The United Nations was founded in what year?
6. Into what political divisions is Switzerland divided?
7. Antimacassars are used on
   a. Tables
   b. Chairs
   c. Stoves
8. True or false: the femur is the thighbone.
9. Name the Roman god whose two heads faced in opposite directions.
10. True or false: George Washington's first inaugural address was made in New York.
11. What stables were cleaned by Hercules?
12. If someone gave you petits fours, what would you do with them?
    a. Eat them
    b. Wear them
    c. Put them in the bank
13. The nectarine is a cross between which two fruits?
14. During whose administration was the Department of Health, Education, and Welfare created?
15. Who was Disraeli's greatest political rival?
16. Name the mother and father of King Solomon.
17. In mythology across what river did Charon ferry the spirits of the dead?
18. True or false: A porcupine is a rodent.
19. Kirman, kilim, and soumak are all different kinds of what?
20. Who received nearly a million votes for president of the United States while serving a prison sentence?
21. What was the nationality of Mata Hari, famous World War I spy?
22. What does "c" before a date mean?
23. What was the first state to secede from the Union in 1869?
24. What king succeeded his son to the throne?
25. Roman, Bodoni, and Gothic are names for what?

The Second Trivia Quizbook

Answers

1. ADVERTISING SLOGANS

Part I

1. G	2. K	3. O	4. F	5. J
6. B	7. L	8. A.	9. D	10. I
11. M	12. N	13. E	14. H	15. C

Part II

1. E	2. L	3. D	4. J	5. K
6. B	7. N	8. F	9. C	10. M
11. G	12. O	13. I	14. A	15. H

2. ANIMAL COLLECTIVES OR GROUPS

Part I

1. I	2. B	3. F	4. J
5. A	6. L	7. H	8. C
9. G	10. E	11. D	12. K

Part II

1. B	2. D	3. C	4. H
5. J	6. E	7. A	8. F
9. I	10. G	11. L	12. K

3. ANIMAL CLASSIFICATION

Part I	1. B	2. D	3. C	4. A	5. E
Part II	1. D	2. E	3. C	4. B	5. A
Part III	1. D	2. E	3. A	4. B	5. C

4. ANIMAL YOUNG

1. I	2. F	3. E	4. K	5. H
6. M	7. P	8. G	9. C	10. J
11. A	12. R	13. B	14. N	15. Q
16. L	17. D	18. O		

5. ANTHROPOLOGY LANGUAGE

Part I

1. L	2. F	3. E	4. A	5. I
6. G	7. B	8. D	9. K	10. M
11. O	12. J	13. C	14. H	15. N

Part II

1. B	2. E	3, F	4. J	5. G
6. M	7. O	8. K	9. D	10. A
11. C	12. N	13. L	14. I	15. H

6. ASTRONOMY LANGUAGE

Part I

1. D	2. F	3. E	4. A
5. H	6. J	7. K	8. I
9. L	10. G	11. C	12. B

Part II

1. F	2. I	3. C	4. A
5. B	6. K	7. L	8. H
9. J	10. D	11. E	12. G

7. ASTRONOMY TRUE/FALSE

1. True
2. True (109 times)
3. False (about 2/3)
4. False
5. True (18.52 miles per second)
6. True
7. False
8. True
9. True
10. False (Mars rotates on its axis in 24 hours, 37 minutes, and 22.58 seconds)
11. True
12. True (11.80 years)
13. True (Ganymede and Callisto)

14. True
15. False (a few occasionally travel much nearer to the sun than does Mars, and still fewer paths lie farther from the sun than Jupiter)
16. True
17. False
18. True
19. True
20. True (1805, 1935, and 2160)
21. False (the sun is)
22. False (about 1/15 the light of the full moon)
23. True
24. True
25. False (about 1/3 the distance between one edge and the center of the galaxy — about 15,000 light years from the edge and about 30,000 light years from the center)

8. BIOLOGY LANGUAGE

Part I	1. J	2. F	3. L	4. C
	5. P	6. B	7. K	8. N
	9. A	10. G	11. D	12. O
	13. I	14. E	15. H	16. M

Part II	1. C	2. H	3. E	4. P
	5. J	6. B	7. M	8. A
	9. K	10. L	11. F	12. O
	13. D	14. I	15. G	16. N

9. BIRDS

Part I	1. I	2. H	3. C	4. A	5. G
	6. J	7. E	8. F	9. D	10. B

Part II	1. J	2. H	3. B	4. A	5. E
	6. C	7. I	8. G	9. F	10. D

Part III	1. A	2. G	3. B	4. I	5. E
	6. H	7. J	8. C	9. F	10. D

10. CHEMISTRY MULTIPLE-CHOICE

1. b	2. e	3. c	4. b	5. d
6. d	7. d	8. c	9. b	10. c
11. c	12. b	13. d	14. b	15. c
16. b	17. b	18. b	19. c	20. e

11. CHEMISTRY LANGUAGE

Part I	1. H	2. B	3. C	4. G	5. D
	6. E	7. A	8. F	9. I	10. J

Part II	1. O	2. G	3. D	4. A	5. Q
	6. M	7. E	8. K	9. P	10. B
	11. F	12. N	13. R	14. L	15. J
	16. H	17. C	18. I		

12. COLORS

Part I	1. C	2. G	3. B	4. F
	5. H	6. A	7. E	8. D

Part II	1. E	2. A	3. F	4. D
	5. H	6. G	7. B	8. C

13. COOKS IN THE KITCHEN

1. A recipe item is allowed to stand or become tender in wine or a highly seasoned liquid
2. Tabasco
3. True
4. Salisbury steak
5. About one day old
6. Bismarck herring
7. Immediately after baking
8. "You shall feed on cherry pie and drink currant wine"
9. Condensed milk
10. Gooseberry wine
11. Flounder
12. To make a bag pudding
13. Yorkshire pudding
14. Worcestershire sauce

15. a. Hungary
    b. France (city of Marseilles)
    c. Poland or Russia
    d. Germany
    e. Italy
    f. The Netherlands

14. COOK'S TOUR

1. c	2. b	3. b	4. a	5. a
6. c	7. c	8. a	9. a	10. b
11. c	12. c	13. c	14. c	15. b
16. c	17. b	18. c		

15. DRUG SLANG

Part I

1. g	2. H	3. A	4. I
5. E	6. C	7. K	8. L
9. J	10. D	11. B	12. F

Part II

1. E	2. A	3. B	4. I
5. H	6. G	7. J	8. F
9. L	10. D	11. K	12. C

16. ECONOMICS

Part I

1. K	2. G	3. B	4. Q	5. L
6. I	7. E	8. A	9. O	10. M
11. J	12. D	13. R	14. N	15. H
16. C	17. P	18. F		

Part II

1. F	2. C	3. H	4. B	5. A
6. G	7. D	8. E		

Part III
1. Agricultural Adjustment Administration
2. American Federation of Labor and Congress of Industrial Organizations
3. Council of Economic Advisers
4. European Payments Union
5. Federal Deposit Insurance Corporation
6. Federal Housing Administration
7. Federal Trade Commission
8. General Agreement of Tariffs and Trade
9. Gross National Product
10. International Bank for Reconstruction and Development
11. Interstate Commerce Commission
12. International Finance Corporation

13. International Monetary Fund
14. National Labor Relations Board
15. Net National Product
16. National Recovery Administration
17. Reconstruction Finance Corporation
18. Securities and Exchange Administration

17. FAMILIAR PHRASES

Part I

1. D	2. I	3. C	4. H
5. B	6. L	7. G	8. A
9. K	10. E	11. J	12. F

Part II

1. G	2. B	3. F	4. A
5. E	6. L	7. K	8. C
9. J	10. D	11. H	12. I

18. FAMOUS ANIMALS

Part I

1. Oscar
2. Tony
3, Spark Plug
4. Rhubarb
5. Sandy
6. Flopit
7. Black Bess
8. Citation
9. Cleo and Figaro
10. Daisy
11. Cerberus
12. Rosinante
13. Champion
14. Alice in Wonderland
15. Manx cat
16. Old Dog Tray
17. Francis
18. Bucephalus, the horse (from Bucephala, the city)
19. Pluto
20. Pegasus

Part II

1. 1. b (the others are marsupial)
2. Rabbits
3. Nutria
4. Madagascar
5. The opossum
6. Tibet
7. Seven
8. Any seal that has external ears
9. A South American monkey
10. The shrew
11. A poisonous snake
12. The hippopotamus

19. FOREIGN, ENGLISH, OR AMERICAN?

Part I	*Part II*
1. Exit	1. Without limit
2. Mayonnaise	2. Each dish priced separately
3. Sold out	3. Fashionable
4. Yield	4. And other things
5. Freight train	5. By virtue of his office
6. Extra fare	6. The end
7. Interchange	7. Pen name
8. Elevator	8. Outstanding
9. Cookies	9. By itself
10. Ground round	10. Private conversation

	1. I	2. C	3. F	4. G
Part III	5. B	6. J	7. H	8. A
	9. K	10. E	11. L	12. D

20. FURNITURE AND HOUSEHOLD ARTICLES

1. D	2. O	3. G	4. K
5. F	6. N	7. E	8. P
9. B	10. C	11. J	12. A
13. L	14. H	15. I	16. M

21. HOMONYMS

1.	a. aye	b. eye	c. I
2.	a. born	b. bourn	c. borne
3.	a. carat	b. caret	c. carrot
4.	a. cent	b. sent	c. scent
5.	a. cite	b. site	c. sight
6.	a. dew	b. do	c. due
7.	a. ewes	b. yews	c. use
8.	a. fain	b. fane	c. feign
9.	a. gnu	b. new	c. knew
10.	a. idol	b. idle	c. idyl
11.	a. knave	b. naive	c. nave
12.	a. liar	b. lyre	c. lier
13.	a. oh	b. O!	c. owe
14.	a. ore	b. o'er	c. oar
15.	a. pair	b. pare	c. pear
16.	a. peak	b. pique	c. peek
17.	a. rain	b. reign	c. rein
18.	a. raise	b. rays	c. raze
19.	a. right	b. rite	c. write
20.	a. roan	b. rown	c. Rhone
21.	a. seas	b. sees	c. seize
22.	a. vale	b. vail	c. veil
23.	a. vein	b. vane	c. vain
24.	a. way	b. whey	c. weigh
25.	a. wear	b. ware	c. where

22. INVENTOR AND INVENTION

Part I	1. C	2. F	3. J	4. G	5. D
Part II	1. E	2. B	3. J	4. F	5. I
	6. A	7. D	8. H	9. G	10. C
Part III	1. E	2. B	3. H	4. J	5. A
	6. D	7. I	8. C	9. G	10. F

23. LANDMARKS OF SCIENCE

1. K	2. F	3. P	4. Q	5. T
6. D	7. G	8. J	9. S	10. O
11. C	12. E	13. H	14. N	15. L
16. A	17. I	18. R	19. B	20. M

24. MATCH YOUR PHOBIAS

Part I	1. H	2. E	3. B	4. K	5. F
	6. A	7. M	8. L	9. C	10. G
	11. D	12. I	13. J		
Part II	1. D	2. A	3. G	4. J	5. L
	6. H	7. M	8. E	9. I	10. K
	11. F	12. B	13. C		

25. MATHEMATICAL TERMS

Part I	1. C	2. F	3. B	4. I
	5. K	6. G	7. L	8. A
	9. J	10. E	11. H	12. D
Part II	1. E	2. I	3. G	4. A
	5. F	6. L	7. J	8. C
	9. H	10. K	11. D	12. B

26. MEDICAL AILMENTS

Part I	1. I	2. P	3. O	4. G
	5. E	6. B	7. F	8. N
	9. M	10. J	11. L	12. H
	13. D	14. C	15. A	16. K
Part II	1. J	2. N	3. G	4. A
	5. F	6. D	7. L	8. P
	9. K	10. O	11. I	12. M
	13. H	14. E	15. C	16. B

27. MATCH THE -OLOGIES

Part I	1. F	2. H	3. E	4. G

Part II	1. G	2. D	3. F	4. H
	6. E	7. B	8. C	9. I

28. NICKNAMES OF AMERICAN STATESMEN

Part I	1. H	2. G	3. L	4. F	5. K
	6. D	7. I	8. E	9. M	10. A
	11. C	12. B	13. J		

Part II	1. H	2. N	3. F	4. L	5. M
	6. J	7. A	8. I	9. E	10. D
	11. G	12. K	13. B	14. C	

29. MORE OR LESS?

1. Penasse, Minnesota
2. Neanderthal period was followed by the Cro-Magnon
3. Cabbage rose (pink), talisman rose (golden yelow)
4. Granite
5. Cirrus clouds
6. Koh-i-Nor (106 carats), Hope (44½ carats)
7. Illinois
8. Anthracite
9. Corinthian
10. MCM (1900), DCV (605)
11. Peanut butter (1 tablespoon = 100 calories, cream (50 calories)
12. Light waves
13. Lead
14. Typhoon
15. Annie Oakley (free pass), Joe Miller (joke)
16. Earth

30. NOBEL PRIZE WINNERS

Part I
1. Chemistry
2. Physics
3. Peace
4. Physics
5. Chemistry
6. Physiology and medicine
7. Chemistry
8. Physics
9. Literature
10. Peace
11. Physics
12. Literature
13. Peace
14. Physiology and medicine
15. Physics

Part II
1. Physics
2. Chemistry
3. Literature
4. Peace
5. Literature
6. Physics
7. Peace
8. Chemistry
9. Physiology and medicine
10. Physics
11. Literature
12. Peace
13. Literature
14. Physiology and medicine
15. Literature

31. A NUMBER OF THINGS

1. Garner, Wallace, and Truman
2. Pride, covetousness, lust, gluttony, anger, envy, and sloth
3. Buddha (Gautama)
4. Famine, death (or pestilence), conquest, and slaughter (or war)
5. Katherine of Aragon, Anne Boleyn, Jane Seymour, Anne of Cleves, Catherine Howard, and Catherine Parr
6. One of them — the number 2 (a prime number is one that cannot be divided, without fractions, except by itself and 1)
7. Belgae (or Gallia Belgica or Belgium), Aquitania (southwestern France between the Garonne River and the Pyrenees), and Celtic Gaul (or Gaul proper or Gallia Celtica)
8. Bulgaria, Hungary, and Romania
9. Prudence, justice, temperance, fortitude, faith, hope, and charity
10. Lloyd George, Clemenceau, Wilson, and Orlando
11. Russia, Austria, and Prussia
12. b
13. Two
14. Van Buren, William Henry Harrison, and Tyler
15. 38 states (¾ of the 50 states)
16. a. The Fourth Crusade
    b. The First Crusade
    c. The Third Crusade
17. Liberia and Ethiopia
18. -273 degrees (-273.16 degrees to be precise)
19. Sweet, sour, salty, and bitter
20. Truman, Attlee, and Stalin

32. OCCULT AND MYSTICAL LANGUAGE

1. G	2. L	3. C	4. A
5. H	6. P	7. F	8. M
9. O	10. B	11. E	12. J
13. I	14. K	15. D	16. N

33. ORIGINS OF NAMES

Part I					
	1 .N	2. J	3. E	4. S	5. P
	6. H	7. B	8. M	9. F	10. A
	11. G	12. L	13. O	14. Q	15. T
	16. C	17. D	18. R	19. K	20. I

Part II					
	1. D	2. I	3. O	4. T	5. P
	6. L	7. G	8. Q	9. A	10. F
	11. N	12. E	13. S	14. J	15. R
	16. H	17. C	18. M	19. K	20. B

34. OUT OF PLACE

1. c (the others are apples)
2. b (the others are laws relating to economics)
3. d (the others were members of the family name of Huxley)
4. b (the others are cheeses)
5. a (the others are observatories)
6. d (the others were associated with archaeology)
7. b (the others were church councils)
8. d (the others can be classified as the size of printer's type)
9. d (the others are grasses)
10. b (the others are herbs)
11. d (the others made up the firm establishing the Pony Express in 1860)
12. a (the otherts are instruments used in astronomy)
13. c (the others were optimists, whereas Cassandra prophesied disaster)
14. b (the others were major battles fought in the Crimean War)
15. f (the others made up the full members of the Six Nations of American Indian tribes)
16. b (the others were members of the House of Merovingian)
17. d (the others are breeds of turkeys)
18. c (the others were members of the family of Medici)
19. b (the others are bones)
20. c (the others were navy men — Whymper was a mountain climber)

35. PHILATELIC TERMS

Part I	1. F	2. G	3. B	4. I	5. H
	6. A	7. E	8. J	9. C	10. D

Part II	1. H	2. J	3. D	4. F	5. A
	6. C	7. I	8. E	9. B	10. G

36. PHILOSOPHY SCHOOLS AND THEORIES

1. K	2. H	3. B	4. G	5. A
6. L	7. O	8. I	9. C	10. E
11. F	12. M	13. J	14. N	15. D

37. QUOTATIONS IN HISTORY

1. Voltaire
2. Lord Acton
3. Francois Rabelais
4. King George III of England (the source is the Declaration of Independence)
5. John Dryden (*Epistle to Congreve*)
6. Thomas Jefferson
7. Rene Descartes
8. Pyrrhus (a Pyrrhic victory is one that is gained at too great a cost)
9. Sir Isaac Newton
10. Plato
11. Socrates (in Plato's *Apology*)
12. Alexis de Tocqueville
13. John Stuart Mill
14. Pliny the Elder (or Gaius Plinius Secundus)
15. the First Battle of Bull Run (or Battle of Manassas)
16. Noel Coward

38. RELIGIOUS GROUPS AND PEOPLE

1. X	2. F	3. R	4. K	5. B
6. Q	7. J	8. I	9. Y	10. W
11. A	12. E	13. O	14. P	15. D
16. T	17. L	18. C	19. V	20. G
21. U	22. M	23. H	24. S	25. N

39. SHAKESPEARE AND HISTORY

1. The Duke of Marlborough
2. The leading actor in Shakespeare's company, builder of the Globe Theatre, and proprietor of the Blackfriars, who played the title parts in the original performances of *Richard III, Hamlet, King Lear,* and *Othello*
3. A generic name for Spanish and Canary wines
4. Numbers (*Henry V* I, ii, line 98)
5. *Venus and Adonis* from Ovid (or Golding's English version) and the *Rape of Lucrece* from Ovid and Livy
6. Brutus
7. Chaucer, Lydgate, Henryson, and Dryden
8. Euripides's *Iphigeneia*
9. The visit of King Christian of Denmark, King James's brother-in-law, to the English court from July 17 to August 14, 1606
10. Archbishop Cranmer
11. a. Bolingbroke's sentence was not reduced until some time after the tournament at Coventry (I, iii, line 211)
    b. Bolingbroke's departure for France and his return to England are reported in scenes apparently taking place on the same day (I, iv and II, i)
    c. Holinshed's story of the deposition of Richard has been considerably altered (IV, i)
    d. Shakespeare made the entry of Bolingbroke and Richard into London occur on the same day, but not so Holinshed (IV, ii)
12. Patriotism, royalty, war, and character

40. SHAKESPEARE AND NATURE

1. Richard II, Richard III, and Old Gobbo in the Merchant of Venice
2. Brutus about a Roman who accepts bribes (*Julius Caesar,*, IV, iii, line 27)
3. Orleans (*Henry IV*, III, vii, line 141)
4. Gloucester (*Richard III*, I, iii, line 70)
5. Ford (*Merry Wives of Windsor*, II, i, line 106), Hotspur (*Henry IV, Part I*, III, i, line 237), Launce (*The Two Gentlemen of Verona*, II, iii, line 6)
6. Falstaff (*Henry IV, Part I*, I, ii, line 72)
7. Portia (*Merchant of Venice*, II, ix, line 79)
8. Clifford (*Henry IV, Part III*, II, ii, line 17)
9. Ariel (*The Tempest*, V, i, line 89)
10. Apples
11. None
12. Iago (*Othello*, I, iii, line 321)
13. Benedick about Beatrice (*Much Ado About Nothing*, II, i, line 214)
14. Oberon (*A Midsummer Night's Dream*, II, i, line 249)
15. Rosemary and rue (*The Winter's Tale*, IV, iv, line 74)

41. STATE MOTTOS

Part I	1. D	2. G	3. B	4. F	
	5. A	6. E	7. H	8. C	

Part II	1. F	2. A	3. C	4. G	
	5. H	6. D	7. B	8. E	

Part III	1. C	2. E	3. A	4. H	
	5. G	6. D	7. F	8. B	

Part IV	1. H	2. F	3. B	4. E	
	5. G	6. A	7. D	8. C	

42. TEXTILES AND FABRICS

Part I	1. F	2. H	3. N	4. C	5. L
	6. O	7. I	8. E	9. A	10. D
	11. B	12. J	13. K	14. M	15. G

Part II	1. M	2. K	3. D	4. I	5. G
	6. N	7. B	8. E	9. C	10. O
	11. J	12. H	13. L	14. A	15. F

43. TRANSPORTATION

1. Winnie Mae
2. The Hudson River
3. An English bomber
4. The Graf Zeppelin, October 1928
5. General Italo Balbo
6. The autogiro
7. Wiley Post, July 1933
8. 24cents an ounce
9. Yes, in 1929
10. 1927
11. Chrysler
12. Standard Oil Corporation of New York
13. Hudson
14. The Pennsylvania Railroad
15. It had triple ignition and 18 spark plugs
16. It was the first aircraft carrier (1922)
17. Planetary
18. Glenn Curtiss
19. Douglas "Wrong Way" Corrigan
20. America

44. UNDERWORLD SLANG

1. H	2. O	3. Y	4. G	5. P
6. R	7. U	8. X	9. Z	10. A
11. J	12. V	13. Q	14. C	15. K
16. E	17. M	18. S	19. W	20. D
21. L	22. B	23. T	24. F	25. I	26. N

45. WHAT DO THEY HAVE IN COMMON?

1. Fictional detectives
2. Dress designers
3. Playwrights
4. Long-distance runners
5. Played Dr. Jekyll
6. Vaudeville circuits
7. Concert pianists
8. Played Charlie Chan
9. Airplane engines
10. Travel agencies
11. Newspaper columnists
12. Members of comedy teams
13. U.S. attorney generals
14. Baseball pitchers
15. Played the devil

46. WHAT IN THE WORLD?

1. c	2. a	3. a and c	4. b	5. c
6. a	7. a	8. c	9. b	10. b
11. b	12. c	13. b and c	14. a	15. a and c
16. b	17. a and b	18. a and c		

47. WHAT'S IN A NAME?

1. William (Harrison, McKinley, and Taft)
2. a. Three
   b. Two
   c. Six
3. Capetians and Merovingians
4. Harold L. Ickes (interior) and Frances Perkins (labor)
5. Premier Paul Reynaud

6. Aristides (statesman), Aristophanes (dramatist), Aristotle (philosopher)
7. Pierre, Marie, Irene, and Frederick (Pierre and Marie won the prize for physics in 1903; Marie won the chemistry award in 1911; Irene and Frederick Joliot-Curie won the prize for chemistry in 1935)
8. King Philip's War (1675-1676), King William's War (1689-1697), Queen Anne's War (1702-1713), King George's War (1744-1748)
9. Louis XIV would meet Louis XI
10. Wild Bill Hickok (or James Butler Hickok)
11. a. Eurydice
    b. Galatea
    c. Cupid
    d. Philemon
    e. Thisbe
12. Jason
13. Vidkun Quisling (the word *quisling* means "traitor")
14. Tariffs
15. Julius (July) Caesar and Augustus (August) Caesar
16. Johnson, Adams, Roosevelt, and Harrison
17. Armagnacs and Burgundians
18. a. France
    b. England (Great Britain)
    c. Spain or France
    d. Scotland or England (Great Britain)
    e. The United States
19. a. The French Revolution
    b. The American Civil War
    c. The Persian Wars
    d. The American Revolutionary War
20. XYZ (French agents so designated in the XYZ Affair famous in American history)

48. WINES, SPIRTS, AND DRINKS

Part I

1. K	2. F	3. B	4. R	5. Q
6. L	7. M	8. I	9. E	10. A
11. N	12. P	13. O	14. J	15. D
16. H	17. C	18. G		

Part II

1. O	2. K	3. Q	4. U	5. C
6. X	7. L	8. E	9. A	10. P
11. V	12. R	13. Y	14. H	15. D
16. M	17. W	18. N	19. F	20. J
21. T	22. B	23. I	24. S	25. G

49. WHO SAID IT?

1. Will Rogers
2. Carl Sandburg
3. Al Smith
4. W. C. Fields
5. Al Jolson
6. Mae West
7. Greta Garbo
8. Joe Jacobs
9. George Gobel
10. Andy Devine
11. The Salvation Army
12. Calvin Coolidge
13. Anita Loos
14. Westbrook Pegler
15. Noel Coward
16. Texas Guinan
17. Huey Long
18. Ethel Barrymore

50. THE WILD WEST

1. c	2. c	3. b	4. a	5. c
6. c	7. b	8. a	9. c	10. b
11. c	12. b	13. b	14. a	15. b
		16. b		

51. WOMEN IN HISTORY

1. Frances Perkins
2. b
3. Peach Melba
4. Madame Marie Curie
5. Mullins
6. Betsy Ross
7. Pocahontas
8. 16th century (Queen Mary the First, 1553-1558)
9. Charlotte Corday after she murdered Marat (French Revolutionary history)
10. a. World War I
    b. Crimean War
    c. World War II
    d. American Revolution
    e. Trojan War
    f. War of 1812
11. Italy
12. Shirley Chisholm of Brooklyn, New York
13. Queen Elizabeth I of England
14. Rebecca (of Sunnybrook Farm)
15. Amelia Bloomer
16. Jacqueline Bouvier
17. Anne Hutchinson (1600-1643)
18. Thais
19. Jane Austen
20. Marie Antoinette (following the execution of Louis XVI in 1793)

52. WRAPUP-ODDS-AND-ENDS

1. c
2. Sardines
3. c, b, a
4. b
5. 1945
6. Cantons
7. b
8. True
9. Janus
10. True
11. Augean
12. a
13. Peach and plum
14. Eisenhower's
15. Gladstone
16. David and Bathsheba
17. Styx
18. True
19. Oriental rugs
20. Eugene V. Debs
21. Dutch
22. About (circa)
23. South Carolina
24. Carol of Rumania ruled after his son, Michael (1930)
25. Typefaces